MW00980086

Crystallization-Study
of
Isaiah

Volume Three

Witness Lee

The Holy Word for Morning Revival

Living Stream Ministry
Anaheim, CA • www.lsm.org

First Edition, January 2011.

ISBN 978-0-7363-4689-4

Published by

Living Stream Ministry
2431 W. La Palma Ave., Anaheim, CA 92801 U.S.A.
P. O. Box 2121, Anaheim, CA 92814 U.S.A.

Printed in the United States of America

11 12 13 14 / 5 4 3 2 1

Contents

Preface

1. This book is intended as an aid to believers in developing a daily time of morning revival with the Lord in His word. At the same time, it provides a limited review of the winter training held December 27, 2010—January 1, 2011, in Anaheim, California, on the "Crystallization-study of Isaiah." Through intimate contact with the Lord in His word, the believers can be constituted with life and truth and thereby equipped to prophesy in the meetings of the church unto the building up of the Body of Christ.

2. The entire content of this book is taken from the *Crystallization-study Outlines: Isaiah (2),* the text and footnotes of the Recovery Version of the Bible, selections from the writings of Witness Lee and Watchman Nee, and *Hymns,* all of which are published by Living Stream Ministry.

3. The book is divided into weeks. One training message is covered per week. Each week presents first the message outline, followed by six daily portions, a hymn, and then some space for writing. The training outline has been divided into days, corresponding to the six daily portions. Each daily portion covers certain points and begins with a section entitled "Morning Nourishment." This section contains selected verses and a short reading that can provide rich spiritual nourishment through intimate fellowship with the Lord. The "Morning Nourishment" is followed by a section entitled "Today's Reading," a longer portion of ministry related to the day's main points. Each day's portion concludes with a short list of references for further reading and some space for the saints to make notes concerning their spiritual inspiration, enlightenment, and enjoyment to serve as a reminder of what they have received of the Lord that day.

4. The space provided at the end of each week is for composing a short prophecy. This prophecy can be composed by considering all of our daily notes, the "harvest" of our inspirations during the week, and preparing a main point with

some sub-points to be spoken in the church meetings for the organic building up of the Body of Christ.

5. Following the last week in this volume, we have provided reading schedules for both the Old and New Testaments in the Recovery Version with footnotes. These schedules are arranged so that one can read through both the Old and New Testaments of the Recovery Version with footnotes in two years.

6. As a practical aid to the saints' feeding on the Word throughout the day, we have provided verse cards at the end of the volume, which correspond to each day's scripture reading. These may be cut out and carried along as a source of spiritual enlightenment and nourishment in the saints' daily lives.

7. The *Crystallization-study Outlines: Isaiah (2)* were compiled by Living Stream Ministry from the writings of Witness Lee and Watchman Nee. The outlines, footnotes, and cross-references in the Recovery Version of the Bible are by Witness Lee. All of the other references cited in this publication are from the published ministry of Witness Lee and Watchman Nee.

Winter Training
(December 27, 2010—January 1, 2011)

CRYSTALLIZATION-STUDY
OF ISAIAH

Banners:

All human beings need the incomparable God,
the coming Christ, the glory of Jehovah
as the center of the gospel for the new creation,
the living and abiding word of God for regeneration
to have eternal life, and the manifestation of the Lord
Jehovah, the revelation of the Lord Jesus Christ.

We must deal with our flesh by the Spirit of life,
give up the world and turn to God by the love of the Father,
defeat Satan through the word of the Son, and
pass through death to die to the self
by the power of resurrection for the Body of Christ.

All who are in Christ and who are one with Christ
to release God's people and to build up God's house
and His kingdom are servants of Jehovah—
a great corporate Christ, the same as the individual
Christ in being the servant of God.

God wants us to learn one lesson—
to stop our doing, taking Christ as our replacement,
and to keep away from the taste of anything
other than Christ.

The Lord Jehovah desires to have as His dwelling place
a group of people into whom He can enter—the church
as a house of prayer and the house of His beauty,
where the glory of God will be seen.

The believers' enjoyment and proclaiming of Christ
as the jubilee of God's grace will issue in the full enjoyment of Christ as the jubilee in the millennium
and in the fullest enjoyment of Christ in the New
Jerusalem in the new heaven and new earth.

**Announcing the All-inclusive Christ,
Jehovah the Savior, as the Glad Tidings**

Scripture Reading: Isa. 40:1-26

Day 1   I. **The all-inclusive Christ is Jehovah the Savior,
the glad tidings (Isa. 40:5, 9; 43:3, 11; 45:21; 49:26;
60:16):**
  A. *Jehovah* means "He who was, who is, and who will
  be" (Exo. 3:14):
    1. God's name is I Am; His name is simply the
    verb *to be:*
      a. *I Am* denotes the One who is self-existing,
      the One whose being depends on nothing
      apart from Himself.
      b. The I Am is also the ever-existing One; that
      is, He exists eternally, having neither begin-
      ning nor ending.
      c. Apart from God, all else is nothing; He is
      the only One who is, the only One who has
      the reality of being (Isa. 40:12-18).
    2. God requires us to believe that He is (Heb.
    11:6).
  B. Jesus is Jehovah (Exo. 3:14; John 18:4-6):
    1. The Lord Jesus is I Am—the eternal, self-
    existing, ever-existing God, the One who is
    everything to us (8:24, 28, 58).
    2. The name *Jesus* means "Jehovah the Savior,"
    or "the salvation of Jehovah" (Matt. 1:21).
Day 2   C. The coming of the all-inclusive Christ as the glad
  tidings is to be announced as Jehovah our God
  (Isa. 40:3), as Jehovah of glory (v. 5), as the Lord
  Jehovah coming with might to rule (vv. 9-10), and
  as a Shepherd feeding His flock (v. 11).
 II. **The word of comfort spoken to the heart of
 Jerusalem is actually the announcing of the
 gospel; the fact that this word is spoken to the**

heart means that it is concerned not with the outer man but with the inner man (vv. 1-2).

III. **Christ as Jehovah the Savior was ushered in by the voice of one (John the Baptist) crying in the wilderness (vv. 3-4; Matt. 3:1-3):**

A. To make clear, or to prepare, the way of Jehovah is to prepare our heart; every part and avenue of our heart needs to be straightened by the Lord through repentance so that the Lord may enter into us to be our life and take possession of us (Isa. 40:3; Prov. 4:20-23; Matt. 5:8; 15:7-8; Luke 1:17; Eph. 3:16-17).

B. To make clear the way of Jehovah is to make clear the way of Jesus, who is the New Testament Jehovah; the way of Jesus is a highway for our God, indicating that Jesus is our God (Isa. 40:3; Matt. 1:21).

Day 3 IV. **Christ as the glory of Jehovah is the revealing of Jehovah (Isa. 40:5):**

A. The glory of Jehovah is the center of the gospel for the new creation (2 Cor. 4:4-6; Heb. 1:3; Luke 1:78):

1. Glory is the expression of God (John 1:1, 14).

2. Christ is the effulgence of God's glory, and this effulgence is like the shining of the sun (Heb. 1:3; Luke 1:78-79).

3. When Christ appeared, the glory of Jehovah was revealed to be seen by the God-seekers and Christ-believers (Matt. 17:1-2, 5; Luke 2:25-32; 9:32; John 1:14; 2 Pet. 1:16-18).

4. To those on whom Christ has shined, Christ is the glory of God and the hope of glory within them (Col. 1:27; 2 Cor. 3:15-16, 18).

B. The gospel is the gospel of the glory of Christ, which illuminates, radiates, and shines into the heart of man (4:4):

1. The illumination, the enlightenment, that makes the glory of Christ's gospel known to us issues from the shining of God in our hearts (v. 6).

2. God's shining in our hearts brings into us a treasure, the Christ of glory, who is the embodiment of God to be our life and our everything (v. 7).

Day 4 V. **Jehovah is revealed through His speaking (John 1:1, 14, 29, 32, 36, 42, 51; 3:34; 7:16-17; 14:24):**

A. The word of God is actually Christ Himself, the embodiment of God, as the gospel of God (Isa. 40:8; Col. 2:9; Rom. 1:1, 3-4, 16; 10:6-8).

B. The Lord Jesus was sent by the Father for the purpose of speaking the word of God for God's expression; in His word, His speaking, God is revealed and presented to us (John 1:1, 14, 18; 3:34; 5:36-37; 7:17; 14:10).

C. The entire fallen human race is like withering grass, and its glory like the falling flower of grass; the believers in Christ were once like that, but the living and abiding word of the Lord has changed their nature, making them living and abiding forever (Isa. 40:6-8; 1 Pet. 1:23-25):

1. Those who receive Christ, the glory of God, as the living and abiding word of God, are regenerated and have eternal life to live forever (John 1:12-13; 3:15).

2. This living word has brought the eternal life into us to regenerate us, and we have received the eternal life for our daily enjoyment (1 Pet. 1:23-25).

3. The Lord's word will stand forever to enliven men that they may partake of His eternal life for their enjoyment (Isa. 40:6-8; 1 Pet. 1:23-25; Rev. 2:7).

Day 5 VI. **In Isaiah 40:9-26 we have the revelation of the Lord Jehovah—the manifestation of the Lord Jesus Christ, the incomparable God:**

A. "Behold your God!" (v. 9):

1. This is the revealing of the Lord Jehovah, the appearing of the very God as the Lord Jesus

Christ, the Savior, in His becoming a man through incarnation (Matt. 1:18-23; Luke 1:35; John 1:1, 14).

2. Jesus, who is Jehovah, is our God; the revealing of Jehovah is the appearing of Jesus (vv. 1, 14; 8:24, 28, 58; Matt. 1:21).

3. Christ is the complete God manifested in the flesh (1 Tim. 3:16):

   a. The Word, who is God, became flesh (John 1:1, 14).

   b. In incarnation Christ is the entire God manifested in the flesh (1 Tim. 3:16).

   c. In Christ dwells all the fullness of the Godhead bodily (Col. 2:9).

4. Such a brief declaration—Behold your God!— is the glad tidings (Isa. 40:9).

B. The Lord Jehovah as Jesus Christ is the Ruler who comes as a mighty One to rule over us, and He is the Judge to either reward or punish us (v. 10; Matt. 2:6; 25:14-30; 2 Cor. 5:10).

C. As the mighty One, the ruling and judging One, Christ comes to be a Shepherd; He cares for His flock by ruling and correcting His sheep and by feeding His flock, gathering the lambs in His arm, carrying them in His bosom, and leading those who are nursing the young (Isa. 40:11; Matt. 2:6; 9:36; John 10:2-4, 11, 14).

Day 6 D. Christ is the Holy One, the eternal God, Jehovah, the Creator of the ends of the earth, sitting above the circle of the earth (Isa. 40:22, 25-26, 28a):

1. As the Holy One, Jesus is unlimited, unsearchable, incomparable, and high; there is no comparison between Him and anyone or anything else (vv. 12-18, 28b, 22a):

   a. All peoples are like a drop of water from a bucket, like specks of dust on the scales, and are nothing, even less than nothing, just vanity, emptiness (Isa. 40:15, 17; Eccl. 1:2; cf. S. S. 1:1).

      b. The proper preaching of the all-inclusive Christ as the glad tidings, the gospel, causes people to realize that they are nothing and that Christ is everything (Isa. 40:15, 17).

    2. The more we realize that apart from Christ we are nothing, emptiness, and vanity, the more we will appreciate Christ, treasure Christ, and seek to be filled, saturated, and permeated with Christ (Phil. 3:7-8).

VII. The prophet's speaking in Isaiah 40—his announcing of the all-inclusive Christ, Jehovah the Savior, as the glad tidings—is an excellent example of preaching the gospel; all human beings need the incomparable God (vv. 18-26), the coming Christ (v. 3), the glory of Jehovah as the center of the gospel for the new creation (v. 5), the living and abiding word of God for regeneration to have eternal life (vv. 6-8), and the manifestation of the Lord Jehovah, the revelation of the Lord Jesus Christ (vv. 9-12).

Morning Nourishment

Exo. **And God said to Moses, I AM WHO I AM. And He said,**
3:14 **Thus you shall say to the children of Israel, I AM has**
sent me to you.
John **Jesus said to them, Truly, truly, I say to you, Before**
8:58 **Abraham came into being, I am.**

The book of Isaiah may be divided into two sections. The first
section is composed of the first thirty-nine chapters, and the second section is composed of the final twenty-seven chapters. Chapter forty, the first chapter in the second section, shows us Christ as
Jehovah the Savior....[Here] we want to see the revelation of the
all-inclusive Christ in Isaiah 40, where Christ is revealed as Jehovah the Savior, as the glad tidings. (*Life-study of Isaiah,* p. 309)

Today's Reading

Now we come to the most wonderful title of God: "I AM WHO
I AM" (Exo. 3:14-15). In verse 14 the Lord instructed Moses, "Thus
you shall say to the children of Israel, I AM has sent me to you."
The Lord's name is I Am. In other words, His name is simply the
verb "to be." We are not qualified to say that we are. We are nothing; only He has being. Therefore, He calls Himself, "I AM WHO
I AM." The Chinese version speaks of Him as "the self-existing
One and ever-existing One." "I Am" denotes the One who is self-
existing, the One whose being depends on nothing apart from
Himself. This One is also the ever-existing One, that is, He exists
eternally, having neither beginning nor ending.

This name, as we have seen, is actually the verb "to be." Only
God qualifies to have this verb applied to His being, for only He is
self-existent. You and I must realize that we are not self-existent.
(*Life-study of Exodus,* p. 59)

He who comes forward to God must believe that God is (Heb.
11:6b). This is very simple. God requires you only to believe that
He is. The verb *to be* is actually the divine title of our Triune God.

Revelation 1:4 and 5 say, "John to the seven churches which
are in Asia: Grace to you and peace from Him who is and who was
and who is coming, and from the seven Spirits who are before His

throne, and from Jesus Christ, the faithful Witness, the Firstborn
of the dead, and the Ruler of the kings of the earth." In these
verses we see the three of the Divine Trinity. God the Father is
called by John in Revelation 1:4 *Him who is and who was and
who is coming.* The One who is coming is the One who will be.
This means that in the whole universe, nothing else is. Only One
is. He is, because He is real. All other things created by Him are
not real. This is why Solomon, the wise king, said that all things
are vanity (Eccl. 1:2). You think you are, but you are vanity. Everything is vanity. The sun, the moon, the living creatures, the heavens, and the earth are all vanities. Only One is. This "is," the verb
to be, implies existing. He is the One who was existing, who is
existing, and who is to be existing. No human language can adequately express what this title *I Am* means.

Paul said that he who comes forward to God must believe that
God is....This implies everything. Do you need God? God is. Do
you need food? God is. This is why we use the word *great* in saying
that Jesus is the *great* I Am. He told us, "I am...the life" (John
14:6a). "I am the resurrection" (11:25). "I am the door" (10:7, 9).
"I am the good Shepherd" (10:11). "I am the bread of life" (6:35).
He is the real food. (*Crystallization-study of the Epistle to the
Romans,* pp. 73-74)

The Lord Jesus is the great I AM. When the soldiers and depu-
ties from the chief priests and Pharisees came to arrest Jesus and
told Him they were seeking Jesus the Nazarene, He said to them,
"I am." "I am" is the name of Jehovah. When the soldiers heard
this name, they drew back and fell to the ground (John 18:4-6).
The name *Jesus* means "Jehovah the Savior." Jesus is Jehovah.
The title Jehovah, denoting the Triune God as the One who is not
only eternally existing but also eternally being, is used more than
seven thousand times in the Old Testament. (*The Central Line of
the Divine Revelation,* p. 14)

Further Reading: Life-study of Exodus, msg.5; *The Central Line of
the Divine Revelation,* msg. 1

Enlightenment and inspiration: _____
_____
_____
_____

Morning Nourishment

Isa. **Comfort, oh, comfort My people, says your God.**
40:1-3 **Speak unto the heart of Jerusalem, and cry out to**
her...The voice of one who cries in the wilderness:
Make clear the way of Jehovah; make straight in the
desert a highway for our God.

Man needs the coming Christ, who is to be announced as the glad tidings. The coming Christ is to be announced as Jehovah our God (Isa. 40:3) and as Jehovah of glory, to be revealed and seen by all flesh together (v. 5). Furthermore, the coming Christ is to be announced as the Lord Jehovah coming with might to rule with His arm, having His reward with Him and His recompense before Him (vv. 9-10). Finally, the coming Christ is to be announced as a Shepherd feeding His flock, gathering the lambs in His arms, carrying them in His bosom, and leading those who are nourishing the young (v. 11). (*Life-study of Isaiah*, p. 142)

Today's Reading

The last section of Isaiah (chs. 40—66) is the kind word of Jehovah spoken to the heart of Israel, His beloved people, which unveils the prophet's vision concerning the redeeming and saving Christ as the Servant of Jehovah and the all-inclusive salvation brought in by Him to Israel and the nations, with the full restoration of all things, consummating in the new heaven and new earth.

Isaiah 40 is Jehovah's word of comfort to Israel. This word is actually the word of the gospel. Verses 1 and 2 say, "Comfort, oh, comfort My people, / Says your God. / Speak unto the heart of Jerusalem,... / That the penalty for her iniquity has been accepted; / For she has received from the hand of Jehovah double / For all her sins." For centuries Israel has been suffering under God's chastisement, but the day will come when this word of comfort, this word of the gospel, will be spoken to Israel.

The New Testament shows that God came to man as Jesus, the incarnated One....For His coming there was the need of a forerunner to usher in the incarnated God to His people. This forerunner was John the Baptist. The New Testament opens with John's ushering, recommendation, and introduction of the incarnated God.

John's introduction was prophesied by Isaiah in 40:3-4. Jehovah the Savior, Jesus, was ushered in by the voice of John the Baptist crying in the wilderness,…"Make clear / The way of Jehovah; / Make straight in the desert / A highway for our God" [v. 3]. To make clear the way of Jehovah is to make clear the way of Jesus. Jesus is the New Testament Jehovah. Jehovah and Jesus are one person. In the Old Testament, the name of Jesus is Jehovah, and in the New Testament the name of Jehovah is Jesus.

We need to consider what Isaiah means by making a highway for our God. To prepare the way of Jehovah is to prepare our heart. Jesus comes with the intention of getting into our spirit, but to enter into our spirit, He must pass through our heart. Our heart is composed of four parts—the mind, the emotion, the will, and the conscience. The human heart is full of valleys, mountains, hills, crooked places, and rough places.

Before we were saved,…in our heart there were valleys, mountains, crooked places, and rough places. Even now we have to confess that our heart is not that straight, not that level. Our heart is still crooked and rough. The highway is a paved heart. Every part and avenue of our heart need to be straightened by the Lord through repentance that the Lord may enter into us to be our life and take possession of us (Luke 1:17).

Our mind may be full of crooked places, and our emotion may be very rough. We may be cold toward the Lord. This is why John was crying in the wilderness to make straight in the desert a highway for our God.…[Our hearts must become] straight and paved, without valleys, mountains, crooked places, or rough places.…This is John the Baptist's crying word to usher in the Savior, who is Jesus as the revealing of Jehovah God. (*Life-study of Isaiah,* pp. 139-140, 310-311)

Further Reading: Life-study of Luke, msg. 7; *The Pure in Heart,* ch. 1

Enlightenment and inspiration: _____

_____

_____

_____

Morning Nourishment

Isa. **Then the glory of Jehovah will be revealed, and all**
40:5 **flesh will see *it* together, because the mouth of Jeho-**
vah has spoken.
2 Cor. **...God who said, Out of darkness light shall shine, is the**
4:6 **One who shined in our hearts to illuminate the knowl-**
edge of the glory of God in the face of Jesus Christ.

The first thing announced in Isaiah 40 is the coming of John
the Baptist (vv. 3-4). Immediately after this is the appearing of
Christ as the glory of Jehovah (v. 5). The glory of Jehovah is the
center of the gospel for the new creation (2 Cor. 4:4-6). Christ is
the effulgence of God's glory (Heb. 1:3), and this effulgence is like
the shining of the sun. The New Testament tells us that Christ's
first coming was the rising of the sun (Luke 1:78). Thus, when
Christ appeared, the glory of Jehovah appeared to be seen by the
God-seekers and Christ-believers. (*Life-study of Isaiah*, p. 138)

Today's Reading

In Colossians 1:27 Paul says that Christ in us is the hope of
glory. Christ is the mystery which is full of glory now. This glory
will be manifested to its fullest extent when Christ returns to glo-
rify His saints (Rom. 8:30). Hence, it is a hope, the hope of glory.
Christ Himself is also this hope of glory.

Christ can be our hope of glory because He dwells in our spirit
to be our life and our person. According to Colossians 3:4, when
Christ our life is manifested, we also shall be manifested with
Him in glory. He will appear to be glorified in our redeemed and
transfigured body (Rom. 8:23; Phil. 3:21; 2 Thes. 1:10). When
Christ comes, we shall be glorified in Him, and He will be glorified
in us. This indicates that the indwelling Christ will saturate our
entire being, including our physical body. This will cause our body
to be transfigured and to become like His glorious body. At that
time Christ will be glorified in us. This is Christ in us as the hope
of glory. (*Life-study of Colossians*, pp. 117, 128)

In the old creation the shining of God was outward. But with us in
the new creation, the shining of God is inward. God has shined into

our hearts. Now the shining, the glory, the illumination, is within us.

God's shining in our hearts results in the illumination of knowing the glory of God in the face of Christ, that is, in the enlightenment that causes us to know the glory of the gospel of Christ.

Many of us know from experience what it is to have the glory of the Lord shining in our hearts. One day, something of the Lord began to shine within us. Before we experienced this inward shining, we were in darkness. This was my situation in organized Christianity for many years. I heard the stories about Christ, and I was taught concerning the cross. But not until I was saved did I experience the inward shining.

In 2 Corinthians 4:7 Paul goes on to say, "But we have this treasure in earthen vessels that the excellency of the power may be of God and not out of us." God's shining in our hearts brings into us a treasure, the Christ of glory, who is the embodiment of God to be our life and our everything. But we who contain this treasure are earthen vessels, worthless and fragile. What a priceless treasure is contained in worthless vessels! This has made the vessels ministers of the new covenant with a priceless ministry. The excellency of the power is surely of God and not of ourselves. This treasure, the indwelling Christ, in us, the earthen vessels, is the divine source of the supply for the Christian life. It is by the excellent power of this treasure that the apostles as ministers of the new covenant are able to live a crucified life so that the resurrection life of Christ may be manifest.

Outwardly we are earthen vessels, but inwardly we have a priceless treasure. This treasure is Christ as the embodiment of the processed Triune God to be in us the all-inclusive life-giving Spirit. This treasure has a power, and this power is excellent. Christ as the life-giving Spirit in us is the One who shines and works. This is the treasure we have in us. (*Life-study of 2 Corinthians*, pp. 267-269)

Further Reading: Life-study of Colossians, msg. 14; *Life-study of 2 Corinthians,* msg. 30

Enlightenment and inspiration: _____

_____

_____

Morning Nourishment

Isa.   ...Surely the people are grass. The grass withers
40:7-8 and the flower fades, but the word of our God will
       stand forever.
John In the beginning was the Word, and the Word was
1:1   with God, and the Word was God.

Isaiah compares fading men of flesh to the word of God [40:6-8].
What will remain among the human race? Everything will fade
and wither except the word of God. This word is actually Christ,
the glory of Jehovah. All men are fading, but Christ as the living
word will remain.

Isaiah 40:6-8 indicates that all men of flesh should receive the
living and abiding word of God to be regenerated that they may
have the eternal life to live forever (1 Pet. 1:23-24). (*Life-study of
Isaiah,* p. 141)

Today's Reading

Jesus, who is Jehovah, is our God. He is the revealing of Jehovah. Isaiah 40:5 says that all flesh will see Him. This is the glad
tidings, the good news.

Verse 5 also indicates that Jehovah is revealed through His
speaking (John 3:34a; 7:17). In the Gospel of John, the Lord Jesus
told us that He was sent by the Father (5:36b-37a) and that He
did not speak from Himself (14:10). He was speaking from His
Father, His teaching was altogether of His Father, and His speaking was the expression of the Father. The more you listen to His
speaking, the more you see Jehovah. John 3:34a says, "For He
whom God has sent speaks the words of God." He was sent by God
for the purpose of speaking the word of God for God's expression.
In other words, His speaking was the revealing of God. When you
listen to Him, you see God. In His word, His speaking, God is
unveiled and presented to you.

Isaiah goes on to say in 40:6-8a that all flesh withers like the
grass and fades like the flower. All flesh, all of mankind, will not
last. First John 2:17 says that the world is passing away. The
world here, according to its usage in John 3:16, refers to mankind,

to human beings. Human beings will pass away, but the word of Jesus will stand forever. There have been many famous people throughout history who spoke, but their words do not abide forever. When they died, their words died with them, but the speaking of Jesus remains forever. Jesus is still speaking, and His words remain forever.

When we hear His word, we see Him. We were saved by hearing His word. Some may say that at a certain time they saw Jesus and were saved. Actually, they did not see Him physically, but they heard His word. His word is just Himself, and He is Jehovah, and Jehovah is God. Thus, we may say that the word is God. In the beginning was the Word, and the Word was God (John 1:1). When I speak, I always exercise not to speak from myself. I exercise to speak the word of the Lord. When we speak in this way, the Lord is present in our speaking, and others are able to see Jesus. When we are under the ministry of the Lord's word, we see Jesus, Jehovah, the Savior, God, the glad tidings. All of these are one. This is why we, the saved ones, like to come to the meetings. In the meetings there is the speaking of the Lord, the word of God. When we hear His word, we see Him.

His word will stand forever to enliven men that they may partake of His eternal life for their enjoyment (Isa. 40:8b; 1 Pet. 1:23-25). When people listen to His word, they are enlivened. When we heard the gospel, we saw Jesus, we were made alive, and we partook of His eternal life for our enjoyment. Peter told us in his first Epistle that we have been regenerated through the living and abiding word of God. As fallen men, we were like withering grass and fading flowers, yet we heard the living word, which is abiding forever. This living word brought the eternal life into us to regenerate us, and we received the eternal life for our daily enjoyment. This is the first aspect of the glad tidings. (*Life-study of Isaiah,* pp. 311-313)

Further Reading: Life-study of John, msg. 2; *The Conclusion of the New Testament,* msg. 22

Enlightenment and inspiration: _____
_____
_____
_____

Morning Nourishment

Isa. Go up to a high mountain, O Zion, who brings glad
40:9 tidings; lift up your voice with power, O Jerusalem,
who brings glad tidings; lift *it* up, do not be afraid. Say
to the cities of Judah, Behold your God!
11 He will feed His flock as a Shepherd; in His arm He
will gather the lambs; in His bosom He will carry
***them*. He will lead those who are nursing *the young*.**

Isaiah 40:9 declares the glad tidings—"Behold your God!" This
is Jehovah's appearing. Jehovah is here, and He is your God. This is
the glad tidings. If you have God, you have everything. If you have
God, every problem will be solved, every lack will be supplied, and
every shortage will be filled. This short word—"Behold your God!"—
is the glad tidings. We should pray adequately to be filled with God,
to receive the infilling of the Holy Spirit. Then when we come to the
meeting, in a sense, we may not need to speak that much. Instead
we can all declare, "Behold our God!" This is the second aspect of
the glad tidings. (*Life-study of Isaiah*, p. 313)

Today's Reading

The revealing of Jehovah is the appearing of Jesus. John told
people that he was not the Christ but the one coming before Christ
to prepare His way (Mark 1:1-8). Jesus, the One coming after John,
would be the appearing of Jehovah. (*Life-study of Isaiah*, p. 311)

In 1 Timothy 3:15-16 Christ is presented as God manifested in
the flesh. This is one of the greatest aspects of Christ for our experience and enjoyment. Not only was the Lord Jesus the manifestation of God in the flesh in the past; the church today should also
be the manifestation of God in the flesh.

God's manifestation was first in Christ as an individual expression in the flesh (1 Tim. 3:16; Col. 2:9; John 1:1, 14). The New Testament does not say that only the Son of God was incarnated.
Rather, it reveals that God was manifested in the flesh, indicating
that the entire God—the Father, the Son, and the Spirit—was
incarnated. Therefore, Christ in His incarnation was the entire
God manifested in the flesh.

According to the Gospel of John, the Word, who is God, became flesh (vv. 1, 14). The God who the Word is, is not a partial God but the entire God—God the Father, God the Son, and God the Spirit. The Word is God's definition, explanation, and expression. Hence, the Word who became flesh—God manifested in the flesh—is God's definition, explanation, and expression in the flesh (v. 18). God was manifested in the flesh not only as the Son but as the entire Triune God—the Father, the Son, and the Spirit. (*The Conclusion of the New Testament,* pp. 3661-3662)

The third aspect of the glad tidings is the Lord Jehovah coming. He comes as a mighty One to rule and to recompense (Isa. 40:10). He is the Ruler who comes as a mighty One to rule over us. He is also the Judge. He will either reward us or punish us. This is His recompense, which is His judgment. Jesus came as the Savior, but in the four Gospels we also see Him as the Judge.

As the mighty One, the ruling and judging One, He comes to be a Shepherd (Isa. 40:11; Matt. 9:36; John 10:2-4, 11, 14). In a shepherd's care for his flock,...his ruling and correcting is his shepherding. In the past, we may have been wild persons who would not listen to the gospel or to the word of God. But in His ruling, Jesus did something to regulate us. His regulating is His shepherding....His regulating shepherds us to bring us into the flock, to get us on the right way, and to adjust us to the proper pace. He is adjusting us not to go too fast or too slow but to take the pace of the flock. Today He is still shepherding us by adjusting us. He directs us, stops us, and urges us on.

As the Shepherd, He also feeds His flock, gathers the lambs in His arm, carries them in His bosom, and leads those who are nursing the young. Among us some are lambs and some are those who are nursing the young. Jesus, our Shepherd, takes care of His entire flock. This is surely a part of the glad tidings. (*Life-study of Isaiah,* pp. 313-314)

Further Reading: Life-study of Isaiah, msg. 21; *The Conclusion of the New Testament,* msg. 363

Enlightenment and inspiration: _____

_____

_____

Morning Nourishment

Isa. It is He who sits above the circle of the earth, and its
40:22 inhabitants are like grasshoppers; who stretches out
the heavens like a curtain, and spreads them out like
a tent to dwell in.

28 Do you not know, or have you not heard, that the eternal God, Jehovah, the Creator of the ends of the earth,
does not faint and does not become weary? There is
no searching out of His understanding.

After [the Lord's]…shepherding, the flock, the sheep, will know
Jesus as the Holy One, the eternal God, Jehovah, the Creator of
the ends of the earth, sitting above the circle of the earth (Isa.
40:22, 25-26, 28a). As we feed a new believer whom we have
brought to the Lord, he will be helped by us to know Jesus more.
He will be helped to know Jesus as the eternal God, Jehovah, the
Creator of the ends of the earth. (*Life-study of Isaiah*, p. 314)

Today's Reading

Actually, Isaiah 40 reveals the steps of the God-ordained way.
We have to get people saved and feed them. Then they will begin
to know that their Savior, Jesus, is the Holy One, the eternal God,
Jehovah, and the Creator of the heavens and the earth. When we go
to visit the new believers, we should speak to them about Jesus in
these aspects. Then they will be fed. They will realize that Jesus is
wonderful,…[that] there is no comparison between Him and anyone
or anything else. As the Holy One, Jesus is unlimited, unsearchable, incomparable, and high (Isa. 40:12-14, 17-18, 28b, 22a).

Isaiah 40:15 and 17 say that all peoples are like a drop of water
from a bucket, like specks of dust on the scales, and are nothing,
even less than nothing, just vanity—emptiness. Perhaps you will
bring a college professor to the Lord and then begin to feed him.…
[He] may consider that he is a very important person with much
prestige. As you feed him, however, he will come to know that he is
like a drop of water from a bucket or a speck of dust on the heavenly scale. Eventually, he will realize that he is nothing and that
Christ is everything. He will realize that apart from Christ, he is

even less than nothing, vanity, emptiness. This will be the result of your visiting him to feed him again and again.

Saul of Tarsus was like this. Eventually, he realized that all things were dung and that only Christ is the excellent One. He even considered the knowledge of Christ to be excellent (Phil. 3:8).

Chapter forty of Isaiah unveils what man really is and what man really needs. The prophet's speaking in this chapter surely is an excellent example of preaching the gospel.

This chapter indicates that man cannot be compared to God, who is great, who takes up the islands as very fine powder, who sits above the circle of the earth, who stretches out the heavens like a curtain and spreads them out like a tent, and who brings the princes to nought and makes the judges of the earth as nothing (vv. 15b-18, 22-26).

Man needs the incomparable God (vv. 18-26). Fading man needs the eternal God, the only One who does not wither and fade but abides forever.

Isaiah 40 presents a marvelous picture of the all-inclusive Christ as Jehovah the Savior. Through His living and abiding word, we have been regenerated. We have been fed by Him to know Him as the Holy One, the eternal God, Jehovah, the Creator of the heavens and the earth. He is unlimited, unsearchable, incomparable, and high. We human beings are as a drop of water and specks of dust. We are nothing and even less than nothing, vanity, emptiness. When we know Christ in this way, we are qualified to wait on Him. We are nothing, and He is everything. Therefore, we do not have any trust in ourselves. We put our trust in Him and wait on Him. He then gives us the eagles' wings to mount up, so that we can run the course of the Christian life without fainting or becoming weary. This is the very Christ presented to us in Isaiah 40. (*Life-study of Isaiah,* pp. 314-315, 140-142, 316)

Further Reading: Life-study of Isaiah, msg. 44; *The Experience of Christ,* ch. 12; *Life-study of Ecclesiastes,* msgs. 1-2

Enlightenment and inspiration: _____

_____

_____

_____

Hymns, #171

1 Lord Jesus Christ, our heart feels sweet
    Whene'er we think on Thee,
  And long that to Thy presence dear
    We soon might raptured be!

    Lord, like the pretty henna-flower,*
      In vineyards blossoming Thou art;
    Incomp'rable Thy beauty is,
      Admires and loves our heart!

2 There is no music adequate
    Thy grace in full to praise,
  Nor there a heart which could enjoy
    Thy love in every phase.

3 Yet, what delights our heart the most
    Is not Thy love, Thy grace;
  But it is Thine own loving Self
    That satisfies always.

4 Oh, Thou art fairer than the fair,
    And sweeter than the sweet;
  Beside Thee, none in heaven or earth
    Our heart's desire could meet.

    * An Old World plant, prized for its fragrant
    yellow and white flowers (S. S. 1:14).

Composition for prophecy with main point and sub-points: _____

_____

_____

_____

_____

_____

_____

_____

_____

_____

_____

_____

_____

_____

_____

_____

_____

_____

_____

_____

_____

_____

_____

_____

_____

_____

_____

_____

_____

_____

_____

_____

_____

_____

_____

_____

_____

Living in the Reality of the New Creation

Scripture Reading: Isa. 40:3-5, 28-31

Day 1 I. **The first thirty-nine chapters of Isaiah, corresponding to the thirty-nine books of the Old Testament, focus mainly on the old creation, whereas the last twenty-seven chapters, corresponding to the twenty-seven books of the New Testament, center on the new creation (2 Cor. 5:17; Gal. 6:15):**

A. Isaiah 40 reveals the announcing of the gospel (corresponding to the four Gospels—Isa. 40:1-5), salvation through regeneration (corresponding to the Acts—Isa. 40:6-8), and transformation (corresponding to the Epistles—Isa. 40:28-31); this is the revelation of God becoming a man through incarnation so that man might become God (in life and in nature but not in the Godhead) through regeneration and transformation as the content of God's eternal economy.

B. Both Isaiah 40 and the New Testament begin with the coming of John the Baptist, who ushered in the expected Christ for the initiation of the new creation (vv. 3-5; Mark 1:1-11).

C. The old creation does not have the divine life and nature, but the new creation, constituted of the believers, who are born of God, does (John 1:13; 3:15; 2 Pet. 1:4); hence, the believers are a new creation (Gal. 6:15), not according to the old nature of the flesh but according to the new nature of the divine life (Rom. 6:4; 7:6).

Day 2 & Day 3 II. **John the Baptist is typified by Elijah (Luke 1:17), who is a type of the Old Testament age with the Old Testament economy, and the Lord Jesus is typified by Elisha, who is a type of the New Testament age with the New Testament economy (4:27); according to 2 Kings 2:1-15,** the age was changed to the new creation by passing through four places—Gilgal, Bethel, Jericho, and the river Jordan:

A. Gilgal was a place where God's people were circumcised to deal with their flesh (Josh. 5:2-9; Col. 2:11; John 3:6; Gal. 5:16-17, 24-25).

B. Bethel is the place to give up the world and turn to God absolutely, taking God as everything (Gen. 12:8; 13:3-4).

C. Jericho, the first city that Joshua and the people of Israel had to defeat when they entered into the good land, signifies God's enemy, Satan (Josh. 6:1-27; Eph. 6:12; Rom. 16:20).

D. The river Jordan, where the New Testament baptism began, signifies death (Matt. 3:5-6, 15-17):
   1. To cross the river Jordan, Elijah struck the water with his mantle, which typifies the outpoured Spirit, the Spirit of power (2 Kings 2:8; Luke 24:49; Acts 1:8).
   2. The Spirit of power dealt with the river of death so that the way was open for Elijah and Elisha to cross over.

E. All this signifies that in order for us to be raptured like Elijah or receive the power of the Spirit like Elisha, and in order for the age to be changed from the Old Testament to the New Testament in our experience, we must deal with our flesh by the Spirit of life (Gal. 5:16-17, 24), give up the world and turn to God by the love of the Father (1 John 2:15-17), defeat Satan through the word of the Son (Rev. 12:11; Matt. 4:4), and pass through death to die to the self by the power of resurrection for the Body of Christ (Rom. 6:3-4; Gal. 2:20; Phil. 3:10; Matt. 16:24).

F. Furthermore, we must "tear our clothes into two pieces" (2 Kings 2:12), indicating that we no longer treasure what we are or what we can do (cf. Matt. 16:24); through all these steps we enter into a new age of the new creation, the age of God's New

Testament economy in grace, which is God doing everything for us by giving Himself to us as our enjoyment (John 1:1, 14-17).

Day 4 III. **John was born a priest, but instead of serving with Zachariah in the temple, he stayed in a wild place, wore wild clothing, ate wild food, and did a wild work; he denied the entire Old Testament priesthood, but his work was the beginning of the priesthood in the New Testament for the new creation (Mark 1:1-4):**

A. The first New Testament priest of the gospel of God was John the Baptist, the forerunner of the Lord Jesus (cf. Rom. 15:16).

B. He preached the baptism of repentance for the forgiveness of sins as the gospel of Jesus Christ; his ministry was "the beginning of the gospel of Jesus Christ, the Son of God" (Mark 1:1).

C. He did not offer bulls and goats as sacrifices (Heb. 10:1-4), but he offered sinners saved through his preaching as sacrifices (Mark 1:5).

D. The New Testament priesthood offers sinners saved into Christ as the main sacrifices; they are offered to God in Christ, with Christ, and one with Christ as the very enlargement of Christ to be a part of the new creation (1 Pet. 2:5; Rom. 15:16; 12:1; Col. 1:28-29).

Day 5 IV. **Isaiah 40:28-31 reveals a regenerated and transformed person who is one with the eternal God and absolutely in the new creation— "Do you not know, / Or have you not heard, / That the eternal God, Jehovah, / The Creator of the ends of the earth, / Does not faint and does not become weary? / There is no searching out of His understanding. / He gives power to the faint, / And to those who have no vigor He multiplies strength. / Although youths will faint and become weary, / And young men will collapse exhausted; / Yet those who wait on Jehovah will renew their strength; / They will**

mount up with wings like eagles; / They will
run and will not faint; / They will walk and
will not become weary":

A. Isaiah 40 presents a comparison between Hezekiah, a godly man who was still in the old creation
(chs. 36—39), and a regenerated and transformed
person in the new creation; the apostle Paul is the
best representative of the kind of person described
in Isaiah 40.

B. The Lord gives power to the faint, and to those
who have no vigor He multiplies strength (v. 29;
Eph. 6:10; Phil. 4:12-13; 2 Tim. 2:1-2; 4:7).

C. To wait on the eternal God means that we termi-
nate ourselves, that is, that we stop ourselves
with our living, our doing, and our activity, and
receive God in Christ as our life, our person, and
our replacement (Isa. 8:17; Gal. 2:20; Heb. 12:2;
Col. 4:2).

D. Such a waiting one will be renewed and strengthened to such an extent that he will mount up with
wings like eagles; as a transformed person, he will
not only walk and run but also soar in the heavens, far above every earthly frustration.

Day 6   E. An eagle signifies the powerful, transcendent
God, and its wings signify the resurrection power
of Christ (the grace, strength, and power of God
applied to us) (Exo. 19:4; 1 Cor. 15:10; 2 Cor. 1:12;
4:7; 12:9):

1. The eagle's wings are the means by which the
four living creatures are coordinated and
move as one (Ezek. 1:11); this signifies that
our coordination is not in ourselves but in
God and by the divine power, the divine
strength, and the divine grace.

2. The wings of an eagle are not only for moving
but also for protection; whatever we do and
whatever we are must be by the grace of the
Lord and the power of the Lord; at the same
time, we are under the overshadowing, the

covering, of the Lord's grace and the Lord's power (Psa. 17:8; 57:1; 63:7; 91:4; 2 Cor. 12:9b).

3. The using of two wings to cover the living creatures indicates that in the coordination we should not display ourselves but should hide ourselves under the Lord's grace (3:5-6; 12:9; Phil. 3:3).

F. May we all be like Paul, who was absolutely in the new creation; with him, the old creation had been terminated, fired, and replaced, and now the new creation is here with Christ (Gal. 2:20; 6:15-18; cf. Rom. 6:4; 7:6).

Morning Nourishment

Isa. The voice of one who cries in the wilderness: Make
40:3-5 clear the way of Jehovah; make straight in the desert
a highway for our God. Every valley will be lifted up,
and every mountain and hill will be made low, and
the crooked places will become straight, and the rough
places, a broad plain. Then the glory of Jehovah will
be revealed, and all flesh will see *it* together, because
the mouth of Jehovah has spoken.

In the Old Testament,...the main thing covered is the old creation, and in the New Testament,...the main thing revealed is
God's new creation. Thus, God's two creations mark the boundary
between the Old Testament and the New Testament....In the
first thirty-nine chapters of Isaiah, the old creation is covered,
including God's chastisement of Israel and His judgment of the
Gentiles, whereas in the last twenty-seven chapters, the center of
Isaiah's prophecy is the new creation.

The coming of the new creation does not involve the immedi-
ate end of the old creation. On the contrary, after the new creation
comes, the old creation remains for a period of time. In the New
Testament, the new creation begins with the coming of John the
Baptist. After that, the old creation remains until it is terminated
at the end of the millennium. The end of the thousand-year kingdom will be the termination of the old creation as well as the com-
pletion, the consummation, of the new creation, as signified by the
New Jerusalem in the new heaven and new earth (Rev. 21:1-2).
(*Life-study of Isaiah*, p. 137)

Today's Reading

History tells us that Isaiah wrote his book during two or three
periods of time. I believe that the second part of his prophecy was
written at a time different from the first part.

The second part begins with a word of comfort spoken to the
heart of Jerusalem (Isa. 40:1-2). The fact that this word is spoken
to the heart means that it is concerned not with the outer man but
with the inner man. In this chapter, the speaking of the word of

comfort to the heart of Jerusalem is actually the announcing of
the gospel. Thus, we may understand the word *comfort* as meaning the preaching of the gospel.The first thing announced in Isaiah 40 is the coming of John the Baptist (vv. 3-4). Immediately
after this is the appearing of Christ as the glory of Jehovah (v. 5).
The glory of Jehovah is the center of the gospel for the new creation (2 Cor. 4:4-6). Christ is the effulgence of God's glory (Heb.
1:3), and this effulgence is like the shining of the sun. The New
Testament tells us that Christ's first coming was the rising of the
sun (Luke 1:78). Thus, when Christ appeared, the glory of Jehovah appeared to be seen by the God-seekers and Christ-believers.

After Isaiah 40 speaks of the coming of John the Baptist and the
appearing of Christ as the glory of God, this chapter tells us that,
like the grass and the flower of the field, all men will wither and
fade, but the word of God remains forever (vv. 6-8). The word of
God is actually Christ as the gospel of God. This word is abiding,
and as the word of life, it is also living. All men of flesh, all withering and fading human beings, should receive Christ, the glory of
God, who comes to people as the living and abiding word of God.
Those who receive Christ as this word of God will be regenerated
that they may have eternal life to live forever (1 Pet. 1:23).

According to Isaiah 40:29-31, those who have received the word
and have been regenerated are now waiting for Jehovah. For us to
wait on God means that we "fire" ourselves, that is, that we stop
ourselves with our living, doing, and activity and receive Christ as
our replacement. Verse 31 says that such a waiting one will
mount up with wings like eagles, signifying the resurrection
power of Christ. He will not only walk and run—he will also soar
in the heavens, far above every earthly frustration. This is a transformed person. Therefore, in this chapter we have the announcing
of the gospel (corresponding to the four Gospels), salvation through
regeneration (corresponding to the Acts), and transformation
(corresponding to the Epistles). (*Life-study of Isaiah,* pp. 137-138)

Further Reading: Life-study of Isaiah, msg. 21

Enlightenment and inspiration: _____

_____

_____

Morning Nourishment

2 Kings **And Elijah said to Elisha, Stay here, for Jehovah has**
2:2 **sent me as far as Bethel. And Elisha said, As Jehovah**
lives and as your soul lives, I will not leave you. So
they went down to Bethel.
4 **And Elijah said to him, Elisha, stay here, for Jehovah**
has sent me to Jericho....
6 **...Jehovah has sent me to the Jordan....**
8 **And Elijah took his mantle and wrapped it together**
and struck the water; and it parted to this side and that,
so that the two of them crossed over on dry ground.

Elijah is a type of the Old Testament age with the Old Testament economy, and Elisha is a type of the New Testament age with the New Testament economy. The age was changed by passing through four places—Gilgal, Bethel, Jericho, and the river Jordan (2 Kings 2:1-8). Gilgal was a place where God's people were circumcised to deal with their flesh (Josh. 5:2-9); Bethel is the place to give up the world and turn to God absolutely, taking God as everything (Gen. 12:8); Jericho, the first city that Joshua and the people of Israel had to defeat when they entered into the good land, signifies the head of God's enemy, Satan (Josh. 6:1-27); and the river Jordan, where the New Testament baptism began, signifies death (Matt. 3:5-6 and footnote 2 on v. 6). To cross the river Jordan, Elijah struck the water with his mantle, which typifies the outpoured Spirit, the Spirit of power (2 Kings 2:8). The Spirit of power dealt with the river of death so that the way was opened for Elijah and Elisha to cross over. All this signifies that in order for the age to be changed from the Old Testament to the New Testament in our experience, we must deal with our flesh (Gal. 5:24), give up the world and turn to God (1 John 2:15-17), defeat Satan (Rev. 12:11), and pass through death (Rom. 6:3-4; Gal. 2:20). (2 Kings 2:1, footnote 1)

Today's Reading

At the time when Jehovah was to take up Elijah by a whirlwind into heaven, Elijah tried to leave Elisha, and Elisha did not let him go, in three steps (2 Kings 2:1-8). The first step was from Gilgal to Bethel (vv. 1-3); the second step was from Bethel to Jericho (vv. 4-5); and the third step was from Jericho to the river Jordan. Fifty sons (disciples) of the prophets went and stood opposite them at a distance. Elijah struck the water with his mantle, and the water parted so that he and Elisha crossed over on dry ground (vv. 6-8).

Elijah and Elisha are both types with much spiritual significance. Elijah is a type of the Old Testament age, and Elisha is a type of the New Testament age. The age was changed by passing through four places—Gilgal, Bethel, Jericho, and the river Jordan.

Gilgal was a place where God's people dealt with their flesh (Josh. 5:2-9). The children of those who came out of Egypt had not been circumcised, indicating that their flesh had never been dealt with. When they crossed the Jordan to begin fighting to gain the good land, they first dealt with their flesh by being circumcised at Gilgal.

From Gilgal Elijah and Elisha went to Bethel. In Genesis 12, when Abraham came out of Chaldea (giving up the world) and came to Bethel, he built an altar to offer everything to God. This indicates that Bethel is the place to give up the world and turn to God absolutely, taking God as everything.

Elijah then led Elisha to Jericho. The first city that Joshua and the people of Israel had to defeat when they entered into the good land was Jericho. Jericho signifies the head of God's enemy, Satan.

Finally, Elijah and Elisha went to the river Jordan, which signifies death. The New Testament baptism, putting people into death, began from the Jordan (Matt. 3:5-6, 13). To cross the river Jordan, Elijah struck the water with his mantle. Elijah's mantle typifies the outpoured Spirit, the Spirit of power. The Spirit of power, which some Bible teachers call the "mantle Spirit," dealt with the river of death so that the way was opened for Elijah and Elisha to cross over. (*Life-study of 1 & 2 Kings*, pp. 80-81)

Further Reading: Life-study of 1 & 2 Kings, msg. 12

Enlightenment and inspiration: _____

_____ _____

_____

Morning Nourishment

Luke ...*It is* he *who* will go before Him in the spirit and
1:17   power of Elijah...to prepare for the Lord a people
       made ready.

4:27   And there were many lepers in Israel during the time
       of Elisha the prophet, and none of them were
       cleansed, except Naaman the Syrian.

2 Kings ...When they had crossed over, Elijah said to Elisha,
2:9   Ask what I should do for you before I am taken from
       you. And Elisha said, Let a double portion of your
       spirit be upon me.

As we consider the significance of all these types, we see that
in order for the age to be changed from the Old Testament to the
New Testament, we must deal with our flesh, give up the world
and turn to God, defeat Satan, and pass through death.

After Elijah was taken up, Elisha grasped his clothes and tore
them in two pieces. Then he picked up Elijah's mantle, which had
fallen from him, returned and stood by the bank of the Jordan, and
struck the water, saying, "Where is Jehovah, the God of Elijah?"
(2 Kings 2:12b-14). The water parted, and Elisha crossed over.

Elisha surely received the spirit of Elijah. However, as we will
see, the Spirit, who at Elijah's time performed great miracles such
as shutting up the heavens, opening up the heavens, and calling
down fire from heaven, acted in a different way through Elisha.
Elisha behaved in a way which was very similar to that of the
Lord Jesus in the Gospels, doing many gracious and sweet things.
(*Life-study of 1 & 2 Kings*, pp. 81-82)

Today's Reading

For three and a half years the Lord Jesus brought His disciples
from the dealing with the flesh (Gilgal), to the giving up of the
world (Bethel), to the defeating of Satan, the head of the demons
(Jericho). Eventually, the Lord Jesus brought His disciples to the
river Jordan. The one hundred twenty who were praying in Acts 1
had all been brought to the Jordan to die with Christ and to be
buried with Him....As a result, they no longer treasured what

they were or what they could do but had torn this "in two pieces." Through all these steps, they were in a position to receive the mantle of Elijah, the power from on high. Therefore, on the day of Pentecost the Spirit of power came upon them. Today we are those who are following the Lord Jesus from Gilgal to Bethel, from Bethel to Jericho, and from Jericho to the Jordan. Through all these steps we enter into a new age, the age of the New Testament, where Christ is doing gracious things.

Elijah's rapture typified the termination of the Old Testament age in God's economy....We are now in the age of the New Testament of Christ, who did and is still doing everything graciously.

The Scriptures say that Elijah will come back again (Mal. 4:5; Luke 1:17; Matt. 11:14; 17:10-13; cf. 17:3-4; Rev. 11:3-12). At the end of the New Testament age, the great tribulation will be a time like Ahab's time, and Elijah will return as the same kind of witness. During the three and a half years of the great tribulation, God will be forced to use Elijah again to burn His enemies with fire (Rev. 11:5). Eventually, Elijah will be killed, and after three and a half days he will rise up and be raptured to join...[all the] overcomers. (*Life-study of 1 & 2 Kings,* pp. 82-83)

If we want to receive the rapture of Elijah and the outer garment of Elisha (the Holy Spirit), we must start from Gilgal and continue until we cross the river Jordan. The Holy Spirit can only descend upon those who are full of the resurrection life. We must not think that since we are born again, we will surely be raptured. God cannot rapture those who are not prepared. We must pass through Gilgal, Bethel, Jericho, and the river Jordan. We must pass through all these places before we can be raptured, just as Elijah did in that day. God has told us that we will be raptured. Now we need to follow our course. We should start from Gilgal and go on until we cross the Jordan. God is waiting for us there! (*The Collected Works of Watchman Nee,* vol. 9, p. 314)

Further Reading: The Collected Works of Watchman Nee, vol. 9, pp. 307-314

Enlightenment and inspiration: _____

Morning Nourishment

Mark ..."Behold, I send My messenger before Your face, who
1:2-4 will prepare Your way, A voice of one crying in the
        wilderness: Prepare the way of the Lord; make
        straight His paths." John came baptizing in the wil-
        derness and preaching a baptism of repentance for
        forgiveness of sins.

Rom. That I might be a minister of Christ Jesus to the Gen-
15:16 tiles, a laboring priest of the gospel of God, in order
        that the offering of the Gentiles might be acceptable,
        having been sanctified in the Holy Spirit.

The ordinances of the Old Testament priesthood had already
been formed and established, but John the Baptist did not live or
work according to this religious and cultured way (Matt. 3:1-6).
Since John the Baptist was born a priest, he should have
remained in the temple [and]…performed the priestly service, to
offer bulls and goats as sacrifices, to arrange the showbread in
the Holy Place, to trim the lamps for the light, and to burn
the incense to God. Instead, he worked wildly, baptizing people
into water. What John did as a work was rough and wild. People
went to John from Jerusalem, all Judea, and all the districts of the
Jordan. He told them to repent for the kingdom of the heavens.
After they repented, he "threw" them into the water. This was a
wild activity. No one in history had ever baptized people into
water until John came.…Instead of serving with Zachariah in the
temple, he stayed in a wild place, wore wild clothing, ate wild food,
and did a wild work. (*The Advance of the Lord's Recovery Today,*
pp. 14-15)

Today's Reading

John the Baptist denied the entire Old Testament priesthood,
but his work was the beginning of the priesthood in the New Testament (Mark 1:1-4). He preached the baptism of repentance for forgiveness of sins as the gospel of Jesus Christ. His ministry was "the
beginning of the gospel of Jesus Christ, the Son of God" (Mark 1:1).
He did not offer bulls and goats as sacrifices (Heb. 10:1-4), but he

offered sinners saved through his preaching as sacrifices (Mark 1:5). John the Baptist brought people to Christ as the One stronger than he was and as the One baptizing the repentant people in the Holy Spirit for imparting life (Mark 1:7-8). The first New Testament priest of the gospel of God was John the Baptist, the forerunner of the Lord Jesus. He was the ending of the Old Testament priesthood and the beginning of the New Testament priesthood. From the time of John the Baptist, the priesthood is no longer busy with animal sacrifices. From that time on, the New Testament priesthood is busy with the preaching of the gospel of Jesus Christ, which is the gospel of God.

The main sacrifices of the Old Testament priesthood were bulls and goats as types of Christ. Now in the New Testament, the main sacrifices are not only Christ but also Christ with the saved sinners. The main offerings of the Old Testament priests were types of Christ, but the main offering of the New Testament priests is Christ experienced by the sinners. The sinners are offered to God in Christ, with Christ, and one with Christ as the very enlargement of Christ. In the New Testament, Christ is still offered to God, not in typology but in experience. Today we do not have a Christ in typology. The Christ that we have is in our experience. We are saved not only in Christ but also into Christ, so we all have been made good sacrifices. The New Testament priesthood offers sinners saved into Christ as the main sacrifices.

The New Testament priesthood is not merely a few individual saints but a universal priesthood, a priestly body, telling out the virtues of Him who called us out of darkness into His marvelous light. This telling out is the preaching of the gospel of God's salvation in all His virtues, to make the saved sinners spiritual sacrifices offered to God for His acceptance. We have to offer these sacrifices every day. This means that the preaching of the gospel of God is the daily life of a priest of the gospel in the New Testament. (*The Advance of the Lord's Recovery Today,* pp. 16, 19)

Further Reading: The Advance of the Lord's Recovery Today, ch. 1

Enlightenment and inspiration: _____

_____

_____

_____

Morning Nourishment

Isa. He gives power to the faint, and to those who have
40:29-31 no vigor He multiplies strength. Although youths
will faint and become weary, and young men will
collapse exhausted; yet those who wait on Jehovah
will renew *their* strength; they will mount up with
wings like eagles; they will run and will not faint;
they will walk and will not become weary.

I believe that Isaiah wrote chapter 40 to give us a comparison
between Hezekiah, a godly man who was still in the old creation,
and a regenerated and transformed person in the new creation.
As chapters thirty-six through thirty-nine indicate, no matter
how good Hezekiah was, he was still in the old creation, and thus
he was fired by God. But in chapter forty we see a different kind of
person—one who is regenerated and transformed, one who has
been fired, who has taken God in Christ as his replacement, and
who is now continually waiting upon the Lord. Such a person
"will mount up with wings like eagles." The apostle Paul is the
best representative of the kind of person described in Isaiah 40.
Let us consider the difference between Hezekiah and Paul and
ask ourselves whether we will be like Hezekiah or like Paul. May
we all be like Paul, who was absolutely in the new creation. With
him, the old creation had been terminated, fired, and replaced,
and now the new creation is here with Christ. (*Life-study of Isaiah*, pp. 138-139)

Today's Reading

The fifth aspect of the glad tidings in Isaiah 40 is that Jehovah
the Savior empowers and strengthens those who wait on Him
(vv. 29-31). We experience this when we prophesy, when we speak for
the Lord. When we prophesy, we are empowered and strengthened.

The Lord gives power to the faint, and to those who have no vigor
He multiplies strength (v. 29). In Ephesians 6:10 Paul said, "Be empowered in the Lord and in the might of His strength." He also
declared, "I am able to do all things in Him who empowers
me" (Phil. 4:13). Christ is the empowering One, so we who wait on

Him will not faint or become weary [Isa. 40:30]. In Christ as the empowering One, we will mount up with wings like eagles [v. 31]. ...[Verses 30 and 31 are] the Old Testament way of describing those who trust in Jesus. The New Testament expresses this in Ephesians 6:10 and Philippians 4:13. Paul also says in Philippians 4:12, "I have learned the secret." He learned the secret of sufficiency in Christ, so he did not faint or become weary. At the end of his life, in 2 Timothy 4:7, he declared, "I have finished the course."

Isaiah 40 presents a marvelous picture of the all-inclusive Christ as Jehovah the Savior. Through His living and abiding word, we have been regenerated. We have been fed by Him to know Him as the Holy One, the eternal God, Jehovah, the Creator of the heavens and the earth. He is unlimited, unsearchable, incomparable, and high. We human beings are as a drop of water and specks of dust. We are nothing and even less than nothing, vanity, emptiness. When we know Christ in this way, we are qualified to wait on Him. We are nothing, and He is everything. Therefore, we do not have any trust in ourselves. We put our trust in Him and wait on Him. He then gives us the eagles' wings to mount up, so that we can run the course of the Christian life without fainting or becoming weary. This is the very Christ presented to us in Isaiah 40.

As the eternal God, Jehovah empowers those who are weary...(vv. 29-31). The *wings* in verse 31 signify the resurrection power of Christ. Those who stop themselves and wait on Jehovah will experience this resurrection power, be transformed, and soar in the heavens.

When we wait on the eternal God, we are terminated and replaced by Him, and then we have Him as our life and power, which is the power of resurrection. This power strengthens us and enables us to mount up with wings as eagles and to soar above the earth. This is the full experience of God's salvation revealed in chapter forty of Isaiah. (*Life-study of Isaiah,* pp. 315-316, 143)

Further Reading: Life-study of Isaiah, msgs. 44, 22

Enlightenment and inspiration: _____

_____

_____

Morning Nourishment

Ezek. **Their wings were joined one to another; they did not**
1:9-11 **turn as they went; each went straight forward. As for**
the likeness of their faces, *they had* the face of a man;
and the four of them had the face of a lion on the right
side, and the four of them had the face of an ox on the
left side, and the four of them had the face of an eagle.
And thus their faces were. And their wings were
spread out upward; two *wings* of each were joined
one to another, and two covered their bodies.

We also need...the face of an eagle. After God brought the people of Israel out of Egypt and led them into the wilderness, He
said to them, "I bore you on eagles' wings and brought you to
Myself" (Exo. 19:4). This indicates that in the Bible an eagle signifies the powerful, transcendent God. God is transcendent, buoy-
ant, and powerful. Nothing can suppress Him, oppress Him, or
depress Him. The more you try to suppress Him, the more buoy-
ant and transcendent He becomes. A Christian has God's life
within him, and this life is transcendent, causing us to have an
expression of buoyancy and transcendence. This is the significance of the face of an eagle. (*Life-study of Ezekiel*, p. 54)

Today's Reading

We need to be like an eagle, not allowing anything to hold us, to
suppress us, or to depress us. This means that we should be able to
overcome both persecution and praise....Some can overcome persecution, but they are unable to overcome people's praise. This
should not be the case with us. Whether we are persecuted or
praised, we need to be...buoyant and transcendent. This is exactly
how the Lord Jesus was in John when the people tried to make
Him king after He fed five thousand people with five loaves and
two fish....John 6:15 says, "Jesus, knowing that they were about to
come and take Him by force to make Him King, withdrew again to
the mountain, Himself alone." He could not be held because He had
the power of an eagle and was therefore transcendent.

If we would be a proper Christian, we should be held neither by poverty nor by riches. Like Paul, we should be able to say, "I know also how to be abased, and I know how to abound; in everything and in all things I have learned the secret both to be filled and to hunger, both to abound and to lack. I am able to do all things in Him who empowers me" (Phil. 4:12-13). Paul's word reveals that he had the wings of an eagle.

In the Bible...the eagle's wings signify the strength and the grace of the Lord Jesus applied to us [Exo. 19:4; Isa. 40:31; 2 Cor. 4:7; 1:12; 12:9; 1 Cor. 15:10; 1:31].

In our Christian life we all should bear four wings on four sides, showing others that whatever we are and whatever we do is not by ourselves and is not of ourselves but of God, so that the excellency of the power may be of God and not out of us.

Each of the four living creatures had four wings, two for covering and two for moving. "Their wings were joined one to another" (Ezek. 1:9a). This joining is for moving.

The Bible reveals that the wings of an eagle are not only for power but also for protection [Psa. 17:8; 57:1; 63:7; 91:4].

The grace, power, and strength of the Lord are both for moving and for covering us. On the one hand, the Lord's grace is the power for us to move; on the other hand, the Lord's power is our protection, our hiding place. We are under the overshadowing of the grace and the power of Christ, and we are under the covering of His power. Whatever we do and whatever we are must be by the grace of the Lord and the power of the Lord. At the same time, we are under the overshadowing, the covering, of the Lord's grace and power.

These moving and overshadowing wings should give others an impression of the Divine Being. We have the four wings of an eagle, giving others the impression that we have God with us as our power and protection. This is the eagle. (*Life-study of Ezekiel,* pp. 54-55, 58-60)

Further Reading: Life-study of Ezekiel, msgs. 5-7

Enlightenment and inspiration: _____

_____

_____

_____

Hymns, #475

1 One with Thee, Thou Son eternal,
     Joined by faith in spirit one,
  Share we in Thy death inclusive
     And Thy life, O God the Son.
  One with Thee, Thou Son beloved,
     Part of Thee become thru grace,
  Heirs with Thee of our one Father,
     We're Thy Spirit's dwelling place.

2 One with Thee, Thou Son incarnate,
     Born with Thee, the Man of worth,
  We, the members of Thy body,
     Sojourn with Thee here on earth.
  One with Thee, Thou Son anointed,
     Sharing too the Spirit's power,
  We in full cooperation
     Labor with Thee hour by hour.

3 One with Thee, Thou Son forsaken,
     Judgment and the curse we've passed;
  We to sin are dead forever,
     Hell beneath our feet is cast.
  One with Thee in resurrection,
     Death can never us oppress;
  Live we in Thy new creation,
     Bearing fruits of righteousness.

4 One with Thee, Thou Son ascended,
     Seated with Thee on the throne,
  Thine authority we share and
     Rule with Thee, Thy rank our own.
  One with Thee, Thou Son returning,
     Glorified with Thee we'll be,
  E'er to manifest Thy beauty,
     One with Thee eternally.

*Composition for prophecy with main point and
sub-points:* _____

_____

_____

_____

_____

_____

_____

_____

_____

_____

_____

_____

_____

_____

_____

_____

_____

_____

_____

_____

_____

_____

_____

_____

_____

_____

_____

_____

_____

_____

_____

_____

Christic as the Servant of Jehovah
Typified by Cyrus the King of Persia,
Israel, and Isaiah

Scripture Reading: Isa. 41:2, 25; 45:13, 1; 48:14; 46:11; 44:28; 41:8-16; 42:1; 43:10; 44:1-5, 21; 46:13; 48:16; 49:1-4; 50:4-9

Day 1   I. **In Isaiah 41 through 66 Christ is revealed as the Servant of Jehovah:**
   A. In the book of Isaiah Christ as the Servant of Jehovah is typified by three persons—by a Gentile king, Cyrus the king of Persia; by God's chosen corporate people, Israel; and by the prophet Isaiah; all three were God's servants in the sense of a type.
   B. Cyrus, Israel, and Isaiah all did the same thing to please God by serving to release God's people, to build up God's house, the temple, and to build up God's kingdom, signified by the city of Jerusalem; thus, they all typify Christ as God's Servant (Luke 4:18-21; Matt. 16:18-19).
   C. All who are in Christ (1 Cor. 1:30) and who are thus one with Christ to release God's people and to build up His house and His kingdom are servants of God; those who are one with Christ have become a great corporate Christ (12:12; Col. 3:10-11), the same as the individual Christ in being the testimony and servant of God:
      1. We need to be one with Christ to release God's people from the captivity of Satan back to the enjoyment of God as their possession; our preaching of the gospel is to release these captives to make them the sons of God, the members of Christ, and the constituents of the new man (Isa. 61:1-2; Luke 4:18-21; Matt. 12:28-29; Gal. 3:26; Rom. 12:4-5; Col. 3:10-11).
Day 2   2. We need to be one with Christ to release God's people from Babylon (apostate Christendom) and the principle of Babylon; anything that is

Babylonian gives Satan the ground to defeat
the people of God (Isa. 48:20; 41:21-29; Rev.
17:3-5; Josh. 7:21).

3. We need to be one with Christ to build up the
church as God's temple and as God's kingdom
(Eph. 2:21-22; Matt. 16:18-19, 24; 1 Cor. 14:4b;
Rom. 14:17-18).

Day 3 II. **Christ as the Servant of Jehovah is typified by
Cyrus the king of Persia (Isa. 41:2, 25; 45:13, 1;
48:14; 46:11; 44:28):**

A. Cyrus was raised up by Jehovah (41:2a, 25a;
45:13a; Acts 3:26a), anointed by Jehovah (Isa. 45:1a;
Luke 4:18a), and loved by Jehovah (Isa. 48:14b; Matt.
3:17).

B. He did God's pleasure on Babylon (Isa. 48:14; 46:11),
symbolizing the Roman Catholic Church (Rev.
17:3-5).

C. He was God's counselor (Isa. 46:11b) to subdue the
nations and have dominion over the kings (41:2b,
25; 45:1b; Ezra 1:2a; Acts 5:31; Rev. 1:5a).

D. As Jehovah's shepherd, Cyrus fulfilled the desires
of Jehovah (Isa. 44:28):

1. Cyrus served God by defeating Babylon, God's
enemy (48:14), which had captured His people
and destroyed the temple (2 Kings 24—25), by
declaring the release of Israel from captivity,
and by issuing a decree allowing the Jews to
rebuild their temple in Jerusalem (Isa. 45:13;
Ezra 1:2-3).

2. These three things are types, signifying
Christ's defeating Satan (Heb. 2:14), releasing
His believers from Satan's captivity (Luke
4:18; Eph. 4:8), and building up the church as
God's temple (Matt. 16:18; Eph. 2:21).

3. In subduing Babylon and releasing the captives of Israel, and in charging Israel and sup-
porting them to build up the temple and the
city of their God (Ezra 1), Cyrus did God's pleasure (Isa. 48:14):

a. God loves Israel, loves His kingdom, signified by the city of Jerusalem, and loves His
house, signified by the temple.

b. It was a matter of love for God to use a Gentile king to do what was in His heart; thus,
God loved Cyrus (v. 14).

Day 4 **III. Christ as the Servant of Jehovah is typified by Israel (41:8-16; 42:1; 43:10; 44:1-5, 21; 49:3; 46:13):**

A. Israel typifies Christ for the carrying out of the
kind word of comfort spoken by Jehovah (40:1-2).

B. Israel was chosen by Jehovah and upheld with the
right hand of His righteousness (41:10).

C. Israel overcame the enemies by Jehovah and rejoiced and gloried in Him, the Holy One of Israel
(vv. 8-16; 42:1a; Rom. 8:37; 1 Thes. 2:19-20).

D. Israel was the witness of Jehovah (Isa. 43:10; Rev.
1:5a; 3:14; Acts 1:8).

E. The Spirit of Jehovah was poured out on Israel for
the blessing of his offspring (Isa. 44:1-5, 21; Matt.
3:16; Luke 4:18-19).

F. Jehovah was glorified in Israel (Isa. 43:7; 49:3;
46:13b; John 17:1; 12:28):

1. Israel is God's servant in the sense of fulfilling
God's desire in His economy to have a corporate expression of Himself for His glory (Isa.
43:7):

a. The people of Israel were to be used by God
to express Him in a corporate way.

b. In this sense Israel was one with Christ as
God's servant (41:8; 45:4; 49:3; Hosea 11:1;
cf. Matt. 2:15).

c. The servant of Jehovah is corporate, and
Israel was part of this corporate servant
(Isa. 41:8).

2. In the present age the church, as the testimony of God, serves God for the expression of
God, the glory of God (Rev. 1:2; Eph. 3:21; Gal.
6:16).

3. The glorification of God is the purpose of our

service; the highest service we can render to
God is to express Him in His glory (Eph. 1:23;
1 Cor. 10:31).

Day 5   IV. **Christ as the Servant of Jehovah is typified by
the prophet Isaiah (Isa. 48:16; 49:1-4; 50:4-9):**
   A. Isaiah typifies Christ as the Servant of Jehovah
   (Mark 10:45) for God's speaking (Deut. 18:15; John
   3:34; 14:24):
      1. Isaiah served God as His mouthpiece to speak
      forth His word, which is the embodiment of
      Himself (Isa. 49:1-4).
      2. Isaiah's prophesying helped in the release of
      Israel and the rebuilding of the temple and
      the city.
   B. In verse 4 Isaiah typifies Christ:
      1. People judged Christ wrongly, thinking that
      His word was nothing and in vain; however,
      Christ was assured that the justice due to
      Him would come from God (1 Pet. 2:23).
      2. God values Christ's word (cf. Matt. 24:35) and
      will reward Him for His speaking.

Day 6   C. Isaiah 50:4-5 speaks of the instruction received by
   Isaiah as a servant of Jehovah; thus, Isaiah typifies
   Christ in his receiving instructions from God.
   D. In the life he lived, Isaiah was a type of Christ:
      1. Isaiah 50:6-9 reveals the life lived by Isaiah as
      a servant of Jehovah.
      2. These verses describe the life lived by the
      Lord Jesus on earth (Matt. 26:67; 1 Pet. 2:23).

Morning Nourishment

Isa. The Spirit of the Lord Jehovah is upon Me, because
61:1-2 Jehovah has anointed Me to bring good news to the
afflicted; He has sent Me to bind up *the wounds* of the
brokenhearted, to proclaim liberty to the captives, and
the opening *of the eyes* to those who are bound; to proclaim the acceptable year of Jehovah and the day of
vengeance of our God; to comfort all who mourn.

[Isaiah 41—66 reveals] Christ as the Servant of Jehovah. As
the Servant of Jehovah, He is typified by three persons—Cyrus,
Isaiah, and Israel. In the book of Isaiah, Cyrus is presented in a
very good and positive sense. God said that He chose Cyrus, loved
Cyrus, and appointed Cyrus to carry out His commission. In Isaiah,
Cyrus typifies Christ. Isaiah, the prophet of Jehovah, also typifies
Christ as the Servant of Jehovah. Israel as the corporate servant
of Jehovah also typifies Christ. Christ is the totality of Israel.

All three were God's servants in the sense of a type. Because
Christ is so great, many types are needed to describe Him. The
Old Testament is full of types of Christ. In the New Testament,
the four Gospels portray Christ in four aspects, but He has many,
many aspects. In the book of Isaiah we can see many aspects of
the all-inclusive Christ. (*Life-study of Isaiah,* pp. 309, 317)

Today's Reading

Cyrus, the Gentile king, Israel, God's chosen people, and Isaiah, the prophet set up by God, all…served to release God's people, to build up God's house, and to build up God's kingdom signified by the city. When Jesus came, He did the same thing. Luke
4:18 says that Christ was anointed by God to release the captives.
He also built up the church as the temple of God and established
the church as the kingdom of God. By this we can see that Cyrus,
Israel, Isaiah, and Jesus Christ were all servants of God doing the
same thing. They are four-in-one, and the first three—Cyrus,
Israel, and Isaiah—are wrapped up with the last One, Christ. In
all the three you can see Christ. In Cyrus you can see Christ;
in Israel you can see Christ; and in Isaiah you can see Christ.

Today we are the servants of God. We need a vision to see Cyrus, Israel, and Isaiah typifying Christ as the Servant of Jehovah. We need to have the realization that we are today's Cyrus, Israel, and Isaiah because we are one with our Lord Jesus Christ. We all are God's servants doing the same thing in the universe— to release God's people, to build up His temple, the house, and to build up His kingdom, the city. Whenever I consider what I have been doing, am still doing, and will be doing to carry out God's good pleasure in this way, I become happy. If we give ourselves to accomplish the desire of God's heart, we are the wisest men on this earth. We have the best job with the best destiny. We need to realize that our job as God's sent ones is the highest job.

Everyone who is one with Christ, including us, is a type of Christ because such persons are part of Christ. All who are part of Christ are types of Christ, who is the Servant of God, and they also are servants of God. All other persons have been terminated, "fired," and put aside by God. We who are one with Christ also have been fired by God, but unlike the unbelievers, we have been replaced with Christ to be one with Him. Furthermore, we who are one with Christ have become a great corporate Christ. This corporate Christ is the same as the individual Christ in being the testimony and servant of God.

What are we doing today? We need to be those who are going out to get sinners. This is what it means to release God's chosen people. In eternity past God chose millions of people, but they all were captured by Satan, typified by that evil Nebuchadnezzar. In Isaiah 14, Isaiah combines Satan with Nebuchadnezzar, the king of Babylon (vv. 12-23). All the sinners are Satan's captives. Every time we bring a sinner to salvation, he gets released from Satan's captivity. If we gain one hundred sinners for Christ, that means we reach one hundred captives for God. (*Life-study of Isaiah,* pp. 323-324, 158, 321)

Further Reading: Life-study of Daniel, msg. 13; *The Vision of the Building of the Church,* ch. 9*

Enlightenment and inspiration: _____

_____

_____

_____

Morning Nourishment

Isa. Come out from Babylon; flee from the Chaldeans;
48:20 with a voice of shouting declare; let them hear this,
send it out unto the end of the earth; say, Jehovah has
redeemed His servant Jacob.
Rom. ...The kingdom of God is not eating and drinking, but
14:17 righteousness and peace and joy in the Holy Spirit.

From chapters forty-one through sixty-six [of Isaiah], Christ is
revealed as the Servant of Jehovah. These twenty-six chapters
cover this one person.... We want to cover the revelation of Christ
as the Servant of Jehovah in chapters forty-one through fifty. In
these ten chapters there are four servants of God—Cyrus, the
Gentile king; Israel, God's chosen corporate people; Isaiah, God's
wonderful prophet; and Christ. They are four, but eventually they
are one, so they are four-in-one.

We need to consider what these servants as types of Christ did
and what Christ as the Servant of Jehovah is doing today. They
surely were one with God to carry out His commission to build
the temple as the center and reality of God's interest on the
earth. Today's temple in the New Testament is the church (1 Cor.
3:16-17). (*Life-study of Isaiah,* p. 318)

Today's Reading

The principle of Babylon is mixing the things of man with the
Word of God, and the things of the flesh with the things of the
Spirit. It is pretending that something of man is something of
God. It is receiving man's glory to satisfy man's lust. Therefore,
Babylon is mixed and corrupted Christianity. What should our
attitude be toward Babylon? Revelation 18:4 says, "And I heard
another voice out of heaven, saying, Come out of her, My people,
that you do not participate in her sins and that you do not receive
her plagues." Second Corinthians 6:17-18 also says, "Therefore
'come out from their midst and be separated, says the Lord, and
do not touch what is unclean; and I will welcome you'; 'and I will
be a Father to you, and you will be sons and daughters to Me.'"
According to God's Word, His children cannot be involved in any

matter containing the character of Babylon. (Watchman Nee, *The Glorious Church*, p. 104)

We all need to ask ourselves whether or not we have made a thorough clearance with today's Babylon. We are here following our Christ, who is the Servant of Jehovah, and He requires us to depart from Babylon and to have a thorough clearance with Babylon. In Joshua 6 the children of Israel gained the victory over Jericho, but in fighting against Ai they were defeated. Because Achan kept a Babylonian garment (7:21), God's people suffered a defeat. Anything that is Babylonian gives Satan the ground to defeat the people of God. Therefore, we must forsake everything Babylonian. If we would serve God as His pure people, we first need to have a thorough clearance of all Babylonian things.

The New Testament speaks of the church as the kingdom of God (Rom. 14:17) and the house of God, the household of God (Eph. 2:19). The house, the dwelling place, is also the household, those who dwell in the house. The church as the household is composed of the sons of God (Gal. 3:26), the members of Christ (1 Cor. 12:12). The church is also the Body of Christ (Eph. 1:22-23) and the new man (2:15). Thus, the church is the kingdom of God, the house of God, the household of God, the sons of God, the members of Christ, the Body of Christ, and the new man. Eventually, the church will consummate in the New Jerusalem (Rev. 21:2). The new man is enlarged to be the New Jerusalem, and the New Jerusalem is the holy city, the tabernacle of God and the temple of God.

We need to see the revelation of the all-inclusive Christ from the types in the book of Isaiah. In Isaiah, God has four servants: Cyrus, Israel, Isaiah, and Jesus Christ, the coming Messiah. What did they do? They built up a city, that is, the kingdom of God. The city is a symbol of the kingdom. They also built up the temple, and the temple is a symbol of God's house with God's people as God's household. (*Life-study of Isaiah*, pp. 180, 319)

Further Reading: Life-study of 1 & 2 Samuel, msg. 26; The Glorious Church, pp. 99-115

Enlightenment and inspiration: _____

_____

_____

_____

Morning Nourishment

Isa. [Thus says Jehovah] who says to Cyrus, *He is* My shep-
44:28 herd, and he will fulfill all My desire, even by saying of
Jerusalem, She will be built, and of the temple, *Her*
foundations will be laid.
48:14 Assemble yourselves, all of you, and hear! Who among
them has declared these things? Jehovah loves him;
he will do His pleasure on Babylon, and His arm *will*
be upon the Chaldeans.

Cyrus was raised up by Jehovah (Isa. 41:2a, 25a; 45:13a; Acts
3:26a), anointed by Jehovah (Isa. 45:1a; Luke 4:18a), and loved by
Jehovah (Isa. 48:14b; Matt. 3:17). He did God's pleasure on Babylon, symbolizing the Roman Catholic Church in Revelation 17. He
was God's counselor (Isa. 46:11b; Heb. 10:7) to subdue the nations
and have dominion over the kings (Isa. 41:2b, 25c; 45:1b; Ezra
1:2a; Acts 5:31a; Rev. 1:5a). He was also Jehovah's shepherd for
the fulfilling of His desire in building up the city (symbolizing the
kingdom) and the temple of God and in releasing God's captives
(Isa. 44:28; 45:13b; Ezra 1:2-3; John 10:11; 5:30b; 2:19; Luke 4:18b).
In all of the above aspects, Cyrus was a type of Christ as the Servant of Jehovah. (*Life-study of Isaiah*, p. 320)

Today's Reading

Isaiah tells us that Cyrus was the one whom God chose, whom
God raised up, whom God called, whom God anointed, whom God
loved, and the one who would do God's pleasure to make God
happy all the time. He was loved by God and worked to please
God, to do God's good pleasure. God's good pleasure is His people,
Israel. Israel was God's counterpart. Jeremiah 2 speaks of the
bridal love, the honeymoon love, between Jehovah and Israel....
Jehovah was married to Israel and had a honeymoon with them.
At that time they both enjoyed the bridal love. It is amazing that
these romantic terms came out of the mouth of Jehovah God. He
fell in love with Israel. God is the Husband, and His redeemed people are His wife [Jer. 3:14].

God loves Israel, loves His kingdom signified by the city, and loves His house signified by the temple. Cyrus took care of these three things.

Because Cyrus was used by God and did many things for God, he was God's servant. God needed someone to defeat Babylon, His enemy, which had captured His people and destroyed the temple. Cyrus was used by God to subdue Babylon. Having gained dominion over Babylon, Cyrus, according to God's desire and at the expiration of Israel's seventy years of captivity, then declared the release of Israel from captivity. Cyrus also issued a decree allowing the Jews to rebuild their temple in Jerusalem (Ezra 1:2-3). In doing these things, Cyrus was surely one with Christ as a servant of Jehovah. These three matters—the defeat of Babylon, the release of Israel, and the decree concerning the rebuilding of the temple—were great matters in the fulfillment of God's economy at that time. These three things are also types, signifying Christ's defeating Satan, releasing us from captivity, and building up the church as the temple.

Nebuchadnezzar, the king of Babylon, did something ugly to God. First, he captured God's people. Second, he burned the temple. Third, he destroyed the city. These three treasures which are in God's heart, His desire, were devastated by Nebuchadnezzar. Thus, throughout the entire Bible, God hates Babylon.

Cyrus came in to release the captives of Israel. He did not want any compensation from them for this release (Isa. 45:13). He supported them and provided a way for them to go back to their fathers' land (Ezra 1). That was God's first desire. Then he charged them to go back to build up the temple of their God. That was God's second desire. He also charged them to build the city, which was God's third desire. God loved Cyrus because he did the things on His heart. What he did touched God's heart.

Cyrus was used by God to release God's captured elect, to build His house, His household, and to establish His kingdom on this earth. (*Life-study of Isaiah*, pp. 320, 152-153, 320-321)

Further Reading: Life-study of Ezra, msgs. 3-4

Enlightenment and inspiration: _____

_____

_____

Morning Nourishment

Isa. But you, Israel, My servant, Jacob, whom I have cho-
41:8 sen, the seed of Abraham My friend.

10 Do not be afraid, for I am with you; do not be dismayed, for I am your God. I will strengthen you; surely
I will help you; surely I will uphold you with the right
hand of My righteousness.

43:7 Everyone who is called by My name, whom I have
created, formed, and even made for My glory.

Cyrus was raised up by Jehovah to subdue the nations and
have dominion over the kings (Isa. 41:2b, 25c; Ezra 1:2a; Acts 5:31a;
Rev. 1:5a).

Christ as the Servant of Jehovah was also typified by Israel for
the carrying out of the kind word of comfort spoken by Jehovah to
Israel (Isa. 41:8-20). (*Life-study of Isaiah*, p. 146)

Today's Reading

Each one of us needs to be today's Cyrus. Like Cyrus, we need
to be birds of prey who go out to gain sinners for God's kingdom.
The saved sinners are our prey. All of these saved ones are the
released captives who have been made sons of God and members
of Christ. How good it is! Such a pleasant work should never tire
us out. We should only know how to make our God happy. God's
charge to us should be sweet and pleasant. If we realize that what
we are doing is for God's good pleasure, we will be happy.

Israel as a type of Christ is more subjective. As the ones chosen
by God, they are God's kingdom, God's house, and God's household. Israel as a type of Christ, the Servant of Jehovah, was chosen by Jehovah and upheld with the right hand of His righteousness. Like Christ, Israel overcame the enemies by Jehovah and
rejoiced and gloried in Him, the Holy One of Israel (Isa. 41:8-16;
42:1a; Rom. 8:37; 1 Thes. 2:19-20). Israel also typifies Christ as the
Witness of Jehovah (Isa. 43:10; Rev. 1:5a; 3:14). Just as the Spirit
was poured out upon Christ, the Spirit of Jehovah was poured out
upon Israel for the blessing of his offspring (Isa. 44:1-5, 21; Matt.
3:16; Luke 4:18-19). Also in Israel, Jehovah was glorified, just as

God was glorified in Christ (Isa. 49:3; 46:13b; John 17:1; 12:28).
Cyrus the king of Persia was working for Israel as Israel's servant. He was not only serving God but also serving them. His
pleasant service sent them back to their fathers' land and provided for them on the way. In the ancient days, it was a long journey from Babylon, today's Iraq, to Jerusalem....Cyrus did everything for them, and they went back to their forefathers' land, the
Holy Land, safely. That was Cyrus's service. Today, on the one
hand, we are Cyrus, and on the other hand, we are Israel.

In Isaiah 41:8 Israel is called God's servant. Israel's being
God's servant is related to God's desire in His economy to have a
corporate expression of Himself...so that He may be glorified.
This is the reason 43:7 says that God created, formed, and made
Israel for His glory. God's glory can be expressed only by a group of
people. Israel is God's servant in the sense of fulfilling God's purpose to have a corporate expression for His glory.

It is easy for us to realize that Cyrus was one with Christ as
God's servant, but it is difficult for us to realize this regarding
Israel. We need to see, therefore, that, apart from Israel, Cyrus
could not have done anything as God's servant. For instance,
Cyrus released the captives, but who were the captives? The cap-
tives were the people of Israel, the people who were to be used by
God to express Him in a corporate way for His glorification. In
this sense, Israel was one with Christ as God's servant. The ser-
vant of Jehovah is corporate, and Israel, having been released by
Cyrus, was part of this corporate servant.

Today the church is the testimony of God in the sense of being
one with Christ as the testimony of God. It is in being such a testimony that the church serves God. For this reason, all God's elect
can be considered servants of God with Christ for the expression
of God's glory. The glorification of God is the purpose of our service. The highest service we can render to God is to express His
glory. (*Life-study of Isaiah,* pp. 322-323, 152-153)

Further Reading: Life-study of Isaiah, msgs. 22-23

Enlightenment and inspiration: _____

_____
_____
_____

Morning Nourishment

Isa. And He has made my mouth like a sharp sword...And
49:2-4 He said to me, You are My servant, Israel, in whom
I will be glorified. But I said, I have labored in vain;
I have used up my strength for nothing and vanity;
yet surely the justice *due* to me is with Jehovah, and
my recompense with my God.

In order to understand Isaiah 49, we need to see the three persons of the servant of Jehovah—Christ (vv. 5-9a), Isaiah the prophet (vv. 1-4), and Israel (v. 3). Both Isaiah the prophet and Israel consummate in Christ. All three are one servant. First, all are Israel. Israel, of course, is Israel, Isaiah was an Israelite, and Jesus Christ was a typical Israelite. Thus, as Israelites they all are one. Second, as a whole, Israel was God's servant, His witness, in the Old Testament. Isaiah as a part of Israel also was a servant of Jehovah. In the New Testament Christ is unveiled as the Servant of God (Mark 10:45) and His Witness (Rev. 1:5). This again shows the oneness of Isaiah, Israel, and Christ as servants of Jehovah. But in the New Testament, our oneness with Christ as servants of God is seen more clearly, because the New Testament says that we are in Christ (1 Cor. 1:30). Together we are one corporate Christ. Since we are in this corporate Christ, and Christ is the Servant of God, we also are one servant of God, one witness of God. This is God's eternal view. (*Life-study of Isaiah,* pp. 167-168)

Today's Reading

Isaiah, the prophet of Jehovah (typifying Christ as the Servant of God for God's speaking—John 14:10), served Jehovah as His mouthpiece to speak forth His word, which is the embodiment of Himself (Isa. 49:1-4). Isaiah spoke for God, but Christ spoke for God much more. In His ministry on earth, the main thing He did was speak for God. Even after He ascended to the heavens, He continued to speak, for He spoke in the speaking of the apostles. The Epistles of Paul, for example, are a continuation of Christ's speaking.

The word of God is God's embodiment. When we speak forth God's word, we speak forth God. We cannot speak forth God without speaking forth God's word. We all need to learn how to speak forth God's word.

According to 49:2a, Jehovah made the prophet's mouth "like a sharp sword" and also concealed him "in the shadow of His hand."

Jehovah made the prophet a polished arrow and hid him in His quiver (49:2b). The words of the prophet were arrows, and his speaking was the shooting of an arrow.

Isaiah also worked as a type of Christ, the Servant of Jehovah, to accomplish God's heart's desire. His prophecy helped in the release of Israel and the rebuilding of the temple and the city.

Isaiah typifies Christ as one made by Jehovah to be His mouth-piece to speak forth His word (Isa. 49:1-2; John 3:34a). I am happy because I am a mouthpiece to speak forth God's word. All of us should be happy in the same way. All of us are mouthpieces to speak God's word. If we are not mouthpieces, we are not servants of God. Every servant of God speaks for God. We must learn to speak Christ for God in many ways and in many aspects.

Isaiah as a type of Christ considered himself as Jehovah's servant, a part of Israel, for His glory (Isa. 49:3; Hosea 11:1; Matt. 2:15). We also need to realize that we are a part of today's Israel. Galatians 6:16 says that the church is the real Israel of God. We are releasing sinners for the building up of the church, and we are the church. When we are building up the church as the Body of Christ, we are building up ourselves for God's glory.

The prophet considered himself as laboring in vain, using up his strength for nothing and vanity (Isa. 49:4a). Nevertheless, he was assured that the justice due to him was with Jehovah and that his recompense was with his God (v. 4b).

Since Isaiah typifies Christ, the word in verse 4 applies to Christ. People judged Christ wrongly, thinking that His word was nothing and vain. However, Christ was assured that the justice due to Him would come from God. God values Christ's word and will reward Him for His speaking. (*Life-study of Isaiah,* pp. 168, 323-325, 169)

Further Reading: Life-study of Isaiah, msgs. 24-25

Enlightenment and inspiration: _____

_____

_____

_____

Morning Nourishment

Isa. **The Lord Jehovah has given me the tongue of the**
50:4-5 **instructed, that I should know how to sustain the**
weary with a word. He awakens *me* morning by morn-
ing; He awakens my ear to hear as an instructed one.
The Lord Jehovah has opened my ear; and I was not
rebellious, nor did I turn back.

"He said to me, You are My servant, / Israel, in whom I will be glorified" (Isa. 49:3). This indicates that Jehovah considered the prophet as His servant, a part of Israel, for His glorification. Isaiah, Israel, and Christ are all for God's glorification.

Isaiah told us that he was sent with the Spirit of Jehovah by Jehovah (48:16b). God did not send Isaiah alone. He was sent by God with God the Spirit. The New Testament tells us that when the Lord Jesus was sent by the Father, the Father sent Him with the Spirit of God (Luke 4:14)....We must have the assurance that when we go to people, the Spirit and Christ go with us. Moreover, Christ is the embodiment of the Father, so the Father goes with us. When we go out to preach the gospel, the Triune God goes with us. We need to experience this just as Isaiah did. (*Life-study of Isaiah,* pp. 168, 324)

Today's Reading

Isaiah 50:4 and 5 speak of the instruction received by Isaiah as the servant of Jehovah—"The Lord Jehovah has given me / The tongue of the instructed, / That I should know how to sustain the weary with a word. / He awakens me morning by morning; / He awakens my ear / To hear as an instructed one. / The Lord Jehovah has opened my ear; / And I was not rebellious, / Nor did I turn back." We should not go to speak to others as professors. We should go to speak as learners, as trainees, as instructed and taught ones. To speak a word to sustain the weary, we must have the tongue of an instructed one. Sometimes I am a little concerned for myself and for the trainers in the full-time training. We may speak like teachers who know something. This actually means that we know nothing. We need to speak with the tongue of an instructed one, a learner. Even though I am teaching, I should teach in humility, considering and confessing that I myself do not know much.

As the instructed ones, we need to be awakened by the Lord morning by morning. This is the real morning revival. He awakens our ear to hear as an instructed one. When the Lord Jehovah opens our ear and speaks to us, we should not be rebellious or turn back. We should take His word and obey. This was Isaiah's attitude as a learner serving Jehovah. This also typifies Christ. The four Gospels show that the Lord Jesus held such an attitude.

Isaiah 50:6-9 shows the life lived by Isaiah as the servant of Jehovah. In these verses Isaiah, as the servant of Jehovah typifying Christ, said, "I gave my back to those who strike me / And my cheeks to those who pluck out the hair; / I did not hide my face / From humiliation and spitting. / The Lord Jehovah helps me; / Therefore I have not been dishonored; / Therefore I have set my face like a flint, / And I know that I will not be put to shame. / The One who justifies me is near; who will contend with me? / Let us stand up together! / Who is my adversary in judgment? / Let him come near to me. / Indeed, the Lord Jehovah helps me, / Who is the one who condemns me? / Indeed, they will all wear out like a garment; / The moth will consume them." These verses also describe the life lived by Jesus on earth (Matt. 26:67; 1 Pet. 2:23). This was not only Isaiah's word but also the word of the Lord Jesus. Isaiah typified Christ in his receiving of instructions from God. In the life he lived, Isaiah was a real type of Christ.

In Isaiah 41 through 50 we can see three servants typifying one Servant. These three servants—Cyrus, Israel, and Isaiah, are wrapped up with the fourth Servant, the all-inclusive Christ. They all are one, serving Jehovah God for His good pleasure to make Him happy in releasing and raising up God's elect to build God's temple and God's city and to set up God's kingdom, which will be enlarged to consummate in the New Jerusalem. This is exactly what we are doing today. (*Life-study of Isaiah*, pp. 325-326)

Further Reading: Life-study of Isaiah, msg. 45

Enlightenment and inspiration: _____

_____

_____

_____

Hymns, #190

1   O Lord, as we consider Thee,
     We worship Thee for all Thou art;
     Thou art so rich, so wonderful,
     So dear and precious to our heart.

         What Thou art meets our every need!
         Our hearts o'erflow with praise to Thee!
         All our desires Thou dost exceed
         And satisfy continually.

2   Thou art the very God in truth,
     The God who is both love and light;
     The God who is to us our life,
     The God in whom we all delight.

3   Thou also art a man indeed,
     A man so fine, so good, so pure;
     A man in whom our God delights,
     A man who can our love secure.

4   Thou even art a lowly slave,
     A slave of God to serve for us;
     Obedient to the cross's death
     That we might be delivered thus.

5   Thou art, beside all these, a King,
     A King in life and love to reign,
     By God anointed with His pow'r
     To rule with us in His domain.

6   Dear Lord, as we remember Thee,
     We thus partake of all Thou art;
     As we enjoy Thyself in love,
     We share Thee as Thy counterpart.

Composition for prophecy with main point and sub-points:

Christ as the Servant of Jehovah

Scripture Reading: Isa. 42:1-3; 50:4-7; 53:2-3; 41:21-29; 43:10-11; 44:8; Matt. 12:18-20

Day 1
I. **The source of Christ as the Servant of Jehovah is His divinity (Isa. 42:1, 6; 49:5, 7-8), whereas His qualification is in His humanity, in His human virtues (42:2-4).**

II. **Isaiah 52:13—53:12 reveals Christ as the Servant of Jehovah not in the Old Testament economy but in the New Testament economy; in the Old Testament, Isaiah 53 is the unique chapter that bears the color, taste, and atmosphere of the New Testament.**

III. **In the book of Isaiah we have a detailed prophecy concerning Christ as the Servant of Jehovah:**

A. As the Servant of Jehovah, Christ is the One chosen and beloved of Jehovah; He is the One in whom Jehovah delights (42:1; Matt. 12:18):

1. Jesus Christ, the Servant of Jehovah, was God's choice among billions of human beings.

2. Because He was God's choice, God delighted in Him; hence, He became the delight of God's heart (3:17; 17:5).

Day 2
B. As the Servant of Jehovah, Christ had Jehovah's Spirit upon Him (Isa. 42:1; Matt. 12:18):

1. Jehovah's Spirit is Jehovah Himself; hence, Jehovah's putting His Spirit upon Jesus (3:16; Luke 4:18; John 1:33) meant that He gave Himself to Jesus and that Jehovah and Jesus, His Servant, are one.

2. When Christ was baptized, the Holy Spirit descended upon Him as the economical power for His ministry; with Jehovah's Spirit upon Him, He announced justice to the nations (Isa. 42:1; Matt. 12:18).

C. As the Servant of Jehovah, Christ did not cry out or lift up His voice (Isa. 42:2; Matt. 12:19):

1. Instead of crying out to make His voice heard in the street, the Lord Jesus was calm and quiet; He never made Himself great (cf. John 7:3-9).
2. In His ministry the Lord Jesus did not strive with others, and He did not promote Himself; He had no fame, and He did not seek to make a name for Himself.

D. As the Servant of Jehovah, Christ would not break a bruised reed or quench dimly burning flax (Isa. 42:3; Matt. 12:20):

Day 3

1. This indicates that He was full of mercy; no matter how much He was opposed, He kept open the door of mercy and grace.
2. Today some of the Lord's people are like a bruised reed that cannot give a musical sound, and others are like dimly burning flax that cannot give a shining light; however, the Lord Jesus will not "break" the bruised ones, nor "quench" the ones like dimly burning flax.
3. The Lord Jesus will select some bruised reeds and dimly burning flax and perfect them so that they become useful in His hand to bring forth justice unto victory (v. 20).

E. As the Servant of Jehovah, Christ was willing to be humiliated (Isa. 50:6; Matt. 26:67).

F. As the Servant of Jehovah, Christ was a man of sorrows, despised and forsaken of men; He was not a man of enjoyment and happiness, for His life was a life of sorrows and grief (Isa. 53:2-3).

Day 4

G. As the Servant of Jehovah, Christ did not speak His own word (50:4-5):

1. Having the tongue of the instructed, He spoke according to God's instructions (v. 4).
2. The Lord Jehovah awakened Him every morning, awakening His ear to hear as an instructed one (v. 4).
3. The Lord Jesus was never rebellious; rather,

He was always obedient, listening to the word
of God (v. 5).

4. Because the Lord Jesus had the ear and the
tongue of an instructed one, He knew how "to
sustain the weary with a word"; such a word
was able to minister life (v. 4a; John 6:63).

H. As the Servant of Jehovah, Christ trusted in God
and set His face like a flint; in fulfilling God's purpose, He was strong (Isa. 50:7):

1. In the matter of fulfilling God's will, Christ
was very strong (John 6:38).

2. As the Lord Jesus was walking in God's way
to fulfill God's will, His face was like hard
stone (Mark 10:32-34):

a. When the time of His death was at hand,
Christ as the Servant of Jehovah went to
Jerusalem willingly, even going before His
followers with a speed and boldness that
amazed them (v. 32).

b. This was His obedience to God unto death
(Phil. 2:8), according to the counsel of God
(Acts 2:23), for the fulfillment of God's
redemptive plan (Isa. 53:10).

c. The Lord Jesus knew that through His
death He would be glorified in resurrection
(Luke 24:25-26) and that His divine life
would be released to produce many brothers
for His expression (John 12:23-24; Rom. 8:29).

Day 5
&
Day 6

IV. **According to Isaiah 41:21-29, Christ as the Servant of Jehovah is for the exposing of the falsehood and vanity of the idols:**

A. Everything except Christ is false, vain, and an
idol (42:8; 43:10-11; 46:5, 9):

1. According to 46:1-2 and 5-7 the idols of Babylon are powerless and useless and cannot be
compared to Jehovah.

2. Anything that replaces God or occupies the
position of God is an idol; today's society encourages people to make idols.

B. In 1 John 5:21 *idols* refers to heretical substitutes for the true God and also to anything that replaces the real God; as genuine children of the genuine God, we should be on the alert to guard ourselves from heretical substitutes and from all vain replacements for our genuine and real God, with whom we are organically one and who is eternal life to us (v. 20).

C. As those who are replaced by Christ and wait on Him to enjoy God's life power in grace, we are members of Christ and servants of Jehovah with Christ and in Christ in a corporate way; as members of Christ, we are types of Christ bearing a twofold testimony (Isa. 40:31; 1 Cor. 12:12):

1. We testify that we are nothing, that we have been "fired" and replaced by Christ, and that Christ is everything to us as our reality, centrality, and universality (John 14:6; Col. 1:18; 2:9, 16-17; 3:4, 10-11; Gal. 2:20).

2. We also testify to the falsehood and vanity of the idols, the head of which is Satan, and to the fact that everything apart from Christ is false, vain, and an idol (Isa. 41:21-29).

3. That Jehovah is the unique God can be proved only by a group of people who are His witnesses (43:10-11; 44:6, 8; Acts 1:8).

Morning Nourishment

Isa. **Here is My Servant, whom I uphold, My chosen One**
42:1 ***in whom* My soul delights; I have put My Spirit upon**
Him, and He will bring forth justice to the nations.
4 He will not faint, nor will He be discouraged, until He
has established justice in the earth...
52:13 Indeed, My Servant will act wisely and will prosper;
He will be exalted and lifted up and very high.

Isaiah 42 reveals Christ (Matt. 12:15-21), the Servant of Jehovah (Mark 10:45; Phil. 2:5-11), as a covenant for God's chosen people, Israel, and a light for the Gentile nations (see footnotes 1 and 2 on Isaiah 42:6). The source of Christ as the Servant of Jehovah is His divinity, His deity (vv. 1, 6; 49:5, 7-8), whereas His qualification is in His humanity, in His human virtues (42:2-4). (Isa. 42:1, footnote 1)

Today's Reading

Christ, the Servant of Jehovah as a covenant to the people of Israel and a light to the nations, has a source, an origin. This source is in His divinity, in His deity, in His being God. He was God from eternity past, He is still God today, and He will be God in the future, so He is the One who was, who is, and who shall be. This is Jehovah....If one is going to do business, he needs the capital. Christ's deity is the basic capital for Him to do business. Jesus, the Servant of Jehovah, is God, and He came from the source of God. His source is in His divinity. Some people may boast about their source, about where they are from, but actually our source as human beings means nothing. In ourselves we are nothing, and we may even say that our source is nothingness. However, the source of Christ being the Servant of God is God Himself.

Now we need to see His qualification in His humanity. In His qualification, He is in humanity. In His qualification, Isaiah said that He did not break a bruised reed or extinguish a dimly burning flax (42:3a). Because the plants in the Old Testament are types of Christ in His humanity, Christ is also typified by a reed and flax. In Exodus 30, Moses used the plant life and its extracts to signify Christ's humanity. Christ is the myrrh, the cinnamon, the calamus, and the cassia (vv. 22-25). His qualification is not depending upon His divinity but upon His humanity. How could Jesus Christ be qualified as a Servant of God? Look at His human virtues. (*Life-study of Isaiah,* pp. 330, 333)

Isaiah 52:13—53:12 reveals Christ as the Servant of Jehovah not in the Old Testament economy but in the New Testament economy, that is, as God who became a man, who died and resurrected, and who became the life-giving Spirit to enter into His elect and dwell in them as the indwelling Spirit. (Isa. 52:13, footnote 1)

In Isaiah 53 Christ as the Servant of Jehovah is unveiled in the New Testament way. When we read the Old Testament through without reading Isaiah 53, we receive the impression of the Old Testament economy. But when we come to Isaiah 53 and read it, the flavor, the taste, is altogether of the New Testament, not the Old Testament. In the Old Testament, Isaiah 53 is the unique chapter that bears the color, the taste, and the atmosphere of the New Testament.

The view of Christ in Isaiah 53 is absolutely different from the human view. We all need to believe Isaiah's report concerning Christ. We need to be enlightened so that we may have the right view and receive the revelation to know Jesus Christ in the God-ordained economy, that is, the New Testament economy. (*Life-study of Isaiah,* p. 385)

In the book of Isaiah we have a detailed prophecy concerning the Lord Jesus as the Slave of God. Not even in the New Testament can we find such a record. By considering the prophecies in Isaiah concerning Christ as God's Slave, we can understand more fully what is recorded in the Gospel of Mark concerning Him as a Slave.

Isaiah 42:1 says, "Here is My Servant, whom I uphold, / My chosen One in whom My soul delights." Jesus Christ, the Slave of God, was God's choice from among billions of human beings. Because He was God's choice, God delighted in Him. Hence, He became the delight of God's heart. (*Life-study of Mark,* pp. 15, 9)

Further Reading: Life-study of Isaiah, msgs. 46-47

Enlightenment and inspiration: _____

_____

_____

_____

Morning Nourishment

Matt.   "Behold, My Servant whom I have chosen, My Beloved
12:18-19   in whom My soul has found delight. I will put My
Spirit upon Him, and He will announce justice to the
Gentiles. He will not strive nor cry out, nor will anyone hear His voice in the streets."

In Matthew 12:18-21 we see Christ as the Servant of Jehovah.
Exodus 3 reveals that Christ is Jehovah Himself, but in these
verses He is the Servant of Jehovah. As the Servant of Jehovah,
Christ is the One sent by Jehovah to serve Jehovah's purpose.

Christ is the One chosen and beloved by Jehovah; He is the
One in whom Jehovah delights [Matt. 12:18a]....As the Servant
of Jehovah, Christ had Jehovah's Spirit upon Him [v. 18b]. When
Christ was baptized, the Holy Spirit descended upon Him and
abode upon Him as the economical power for His ministry. With
Jehovah's Spirit upon Him, He announced justice to the Gentiles.
The word *justice* here means "righteousness" or "righteous judg-
ment." A righteous judgment is a decision for the right things. The
Lord Jesus proclaimed all the right decisions for the Gentiles.
(*The Conclusion of the New Testament*, p. 2797)

Today's Reading

[In Isaiah 42:1] Jehovah's Spirit is Jehovah Himself. Hence,
Jehovah's putting His Spirit upon Jesus (Matt. 3:16; Luke 4:18a;
John 1:33) meant that He gave Himself to Jesus and that Jeho-
vah and Jesus, His Servant, are one. (Isa. 42:1, footnote 2)

Matthew 12:19 says, "He will not strive nor cry out, nor will
anyone hear His voice in the streets." This means that the Lord
did not shout or make noise. Instead of crying out to make His
voice known in the streets, He was calm and quiet.

Verse 19 indicates that, as the Servant of Jehovah, Christ was
no longer free to minister openly. On the contrary, because He had
been rejected, He had to hide Himself. As the context of Matthew 12 makes clear, the reason for the rejection and the cause of
the Lord's hiding Himself was His breaking of the religious regu-
lations. This was due to the Lord's caring for His headship and for

the members of His Body. (*The Conclusion of the New Testament,* p. 2798)

When the Lord Jesus was living on earth, He never made Himself great. Rather, He always kept Himself small. This is what it means to say that He did not cry out, lift up His voice, or make His voice heard in the street. (*Life-study of Isaiah,* p. 149)

Isaiah 42:1-3 prophesies that in His ministry, His service, Christ would be Jehovah's Servant, not striving nor crying out, not breaking a bruised reed nor quenching the smoking flax. This prophecy is fulfilled in Matthew 12:17-21. Matthew 12:19 says of Christ, "He will not strive nor cry out, nor will anyone hear His voice in the streets." In His ministry the Lord did not strive with others, and He did not promote Himself. He did not seek to make Himself known to people on the streets. He had no fame, and He made no name for Himself. In a sense He was very hidden. When the Lord Jesus was living on earth, He never made Himself great. Rather, He always kept Himself small. We should be hidden and concealed all the time as Christians. If we would enjoy Christ, we should remain small, concealed, and hidden.

Matthew 12:20 goes on to say, in fulfillment of Isaiah 42:3, "A bruised reed He will not break, and smoking flax He will not quench." Not only did Christ make no noise in the streets; He did not break a bruised reed nor quench a smoking flax. This indicates that He was full of mercy. The Jews often made flutes of reeds. When a reed was bruised and no longer useful as a musical instrument, they broke it. They also made torches of flax to burn with oil. The oil ran out, the flax smoked, and they quenched it. Some of the Lord's people are like a bruised reed that cannot give a musical sound; others are like smoking flax that cannot give a shining light. Yet the Lord will not "break" the bruised ones who cannot give a musical sound, nor "quench" the ones like smoking flax that cannot give a shining light. (*The Conclusion of the New Testament,* pp. 378-379)

Further Reading: The Conclusion of the New Testament, msgs. 35, 270

Enlightenment and inspiration: _____

_____

_____

_____

Morning Nourishment

Isa. I gave my back to those who strike *me* and my cheeks
50:6 to those who pluck out *the hair;* I did not hide my face
from humiliation and spitting.
53:6 We all like sheep have gone astray; each of us has
turned to his own way, and Jehovah has caused the
iniquity of us all to fall on Him.

In His humanity, He did not cry out, lift up His voice, or make
His voice heard in the street (Isa. 42:2). To be quiet indicates a
kind of victory. If a person is condemned and scolded, and yet still
remains quiet and does not argue, that is a victory. If I do not lift
up my voice, that is a victory. This kind of victory is a qualification....Young people want their voice to be heard by everyone. Isaiah tells us, however, that Christ in His humanity did not make
His voice heard in the street. (*Life-study of Isaiah,* pp. 333-334)

Today's Reading

"A bruised reed He will not break, and smoking flax He will
not quench until He brings forth justice unto victory" [Matt. 12:20].
As the Servant of Jehovah, Christ will not break a bruised reed
nor quench smoking flax. This indicates that while He was being
rejected and opposed, He was still full of mercy. Those who were
opposing Him were like bruised reeds and smoking flax, but the
Lord Jesus was still merciful toward them....Even those who had
become bruised reeds He would not break, and those who had become smoking flax He would not quench. Rather, He kept open to
them the door of mercy and grace.

As the merciful Servant of Jehovah, He would use some of
those who are as bruised reeds and smoking flax to bring forth
justice unto victory. If we think that no one is useful except ourselves, we cannot carry out the Lord's work. The Lord would
select some bruised reeds and smoking flax. He would perfect
them so that they could become useful in His hand to bring forth
justice unto victory. No matter how much He is opposed, He, the
Servant of Jehovah, is still merciful. (*The Conclusion of the New
Testament,* pp. 2798-2799)

Isaiah 49:7 says, "Thus says Jehovah, / The Redeemer of Israel, His Holy One, / To the despised One, the One abhorred by the nation, / The One subjected to tyrants." According to this verse, the Lord Jesus was despised by man, He was abhorred by the nation, and He was the…one subjected to tyrants. The Lord was a Slave kept in subjection, in slavery, by tyrants. (*Life-study of Mark,* p. 11)

Christ was also a man of sorrows despised and rejected of men (Isa. 53:3; Psa. 22:6-7; Luke 22:28; 23:11; Matt. 27:39). He was not a man of enjoyment, happiness, or blessing. As we consider Isaiah 53, Psalm 22, Luke 22, and Matthew 27, we see a portrait of Christ as a despised man of sorrows.

Isaiah 50:6 prophesies of Christ as the One willing to be humiliated: "I gave my back to those who strike me / And my cheeks to those who pluck out the hair; / I did not hide my face / From humiliation and spitting." This word is fulfilled in Matthew 26:67: "They spat in His face and beat Him with their fists, and others slapped Him."

According to Psalm 69:9b, the reproaches of those who reproached God would fall upon Christ: "The reproaches of those who reproach you have fallen on me." Christ suffered not only for us but even for God. He suffered as God's Substitute, for the reproaches of those who reproached God fell upon Christ. Hence, Christ was not only our Substitute bearing our problems, but was also God's Substitute bearing God's problems. In Romans 15:3 Paul quotes the prophecy in Psalm 69:9b in order to encourage the saints to bear the problems of others just as Christ bore God's problems.

If you consider the matters we have covered thus far concerning the person of Christ in the fulfillment of the Old Testament prophecies, you will see a portrait of who Christ is and what He is. All these matters are related to Christ's coming to dispense God into His chosen people. Every aspect of Christ's person prophesied in the Old Testament and fulfilled in the New is for this purpose. (*The Conclusion of the New Testament,* pp. 379-380)

Further Reading: Life-study of Matthew, msgs. 24, 70

Enlightenment and inspiration: _____
_____
_____
_____

Morning Nourishment

Isa. The Lord Jehovah has given me the tongue of the in-
50:4-5 structed, that I should know how to sustain the weary
with a word. He awakens *me* morning by morning;
He awakens my ear to hear as an instructed one. The
Lord Jehovah has opened my ear; and I was not
rebellious, nor did I turn back.

Isaiah 50:4-9 describes the instruction the servant of Jehovah (Isaiah typifying Christ) received and the life he lived.

[Verses 4 and 5 refer] to Isaiah as a type of Christ as the Servant of Jehovah....Christ as the Servant of Jehovah was instructed not by man but by God. Christ did not speak His own word but spoke according to God's instructions. He thus learned how to sustain the weary ones, the weak ones, with a word. Jehovah awakened Him every morning. This indicates that every day the Lord Jesus had a morning revival. Furthermore, the Lord was never rebellious; rather, He was always obedient, listening to the word of God. (*Life-study of Isaiah*, pp. 173-174)

Today's Reading

From Isaiah 50:4 we see that as the Slave of God the Lord was given the tongue of the instructed: "The Lord Jehovah has given me / The tongue of the instructed, / That I should know how to sustain the weary with a word. / He awakens me morning by morning; / He awakens my ear / To hear as an instructed one." Although as a Slave, the Lord was not a teaching one, He was nonetheless given the tongue of the instructed. He was instructed by God to know how to sustain a weary one with a word. Because He had been instructed by God, He could sustain a weary one by giving him a single word. Such a word is able to minister life more than a long message. (*Life-study of Mark*, p. 12)

If a brother has a problem, we need to pray for him and seek the Lord for a timely word to speak to him....In order to have such a word, we need the tongue of the instructed, the tongue of the one dealt with by the Lord (Isa. 50:4). If we have been dealt with by the Lord, we will have a tongue that can offer a word to rescue

others and sustain the weary ones....Such a tongue is not that of
a teacher, a professor, or a learned one but of the instructed, the
taught one, the one who has been disciplined by the Lord....The
proper speaking comes from the proper hearing. If we do not listen to the Lord in His dealings with us, it will be difficult for us to
speak a timely word to sustain the weary ones. (*The Normal Way
of Fruit-bearing and Shepherding for the Building Up of the Church,*
pp. 31-32)

Isaiah 50:7 says, "The Lord Jehovah helps me; / Therefore I
have not been dishonored; / Therefore I have set my face like a
flint, / And I know that I will not be put to shame." Here we see
that the Lord trusted in God and set His face like a flint. As the
Lord Jesus was walking in God's way to fulfill God's will, His face
was like a hard stone. In the matter of fulfilling God's will He was
very strong. (*Life-study of Mark,* pp. 12-13)

The Slave-Savior had predicted His death and resurrection
twice already (Mark 8:31; 9:31). Since the time for His death was
at hand (see footnote 1 on 10:1), He went to Jerusalem willingly,
even going before His followers with a speed and boldness that
amazed them (v. 32). This was His obedience to God unto death
(Phil. 2:8), according to the counsel of God (Acts 2:23), for the fulfillment of God's redemptive plan (Isa. 53:10). The Slave-Savior
knew that through His death He would be glorified in resurrection (Luke 24:25-26) and that His divine life would be released to
produce many brothers for His expression (John 12:23-24; Rom.
8:29). For the joy set before Him, He despised the shame (Heb.
12:2) and volunteered to be delivered to the Satan-usurped leaders of the Jews and to be condemned by them to death. For this,
God exalted Him to the heavens, seated Him at His right hand
(Mark 16:19; Acts 2:33-35), bestowed on Him the name which is
above every name (Phil. 2:9-10), made Him both Lord and Christ
(Acts 2:36), and crowned Him with glory and honor (Heb. 2:9).
(Mark 10:33, footnote 1)

Further Reading: Life-study of Mark, msgs. 1-2

Enlightenment and inspiration: _____

_____
_____
_____

Morning Nourishment

Isa. I am Jehovah, that is My name, and I will not give My
42:8 glory to another, nor My praise to idols.
1 John And we know that the Son of God has come and has
5:20-21 given us an understanding that we might know Him
who is true; and we are in Him who is true, in His Son
Jesus Christ. This is the true God and eternal life. Little children, guard yourselves from idols.

In [Isaiah 40], Christ is the replacement for everyone. Since
we have been replaced by Christ, we must realize that we are
nothing—a drop from a bucket, specks of dust on the scales (v. 15).
God Himself is the only One in the universe who remains forever.

Anyone who is replaced by Christ and waits on Him to enjoy
God's life power in grace is a servant of Jehovah. For this reason,
in this book Cyrus, Israel, and Isaiah are types of Christ as the
Servant of Jehovah. They are not servants of Jehovah apart from
Christ, but they are servants with Christ and in Christ in a corpo-
rate way. In this sense, Cyrus, Israel, and Isaiah become Christ.
(*Life-study of Isaiah*, pp. 146-147)

Today's Reading

Today, as members of Christ, we also are types of Christ....On
the positive side, we are types of Christ for the purpose of carrying
out Jehovah's kind word of comfort (Isa. 41:8-20), which is the gospel as His testimony. On the negative side, we are types of Christ
for the purpose of exposing the falsehood and vanity of the idols
(41:21-29). This is the New Testament testimony. We testify two
things: 1) that Christ is our reality, centrality, and universality
and that we are part of Him, and 2) that everything except Christ
is false, vain, and an idol. As types of Christ, we testify that we are
nothing, that we have been fired and replaced with Christ, and
that Christ is everything to us. We also testify to the falsehood
and vanity of the idols, the head of which is Satan.

According to 46:1-2 and 5-7, the idols of Babylon are powerless
and useless and cannot be compared to Jehovah. Furthermore,
the idols are a burden for Israel to carry in their coming captivity.

Concerning this, 46:1 and 2 say, "Bel has bowed down; Nebo stoops; / Their idols are on beasts and cattle; / The things which you carry are a burden, / A load for a weary beast. / They stoop and have bowed down together; / They are not able to escape the burden; / But they themselves have gone into captivity." Bel was one of the gods of the Babylonians.

Anything that replaces God or occupies the position of God is an idol as a burden to the worshipper. Today's human society encourages people to make idols. A person, education, or a high position with a company can all become idols to us. Eventually, every idol will not help us but instead will become a burden that we must carry. (*Life-study of Isaiah,* pp. 147, 161-162)

In 1 John 5:21 John goes on to conclude "Little children, guard yourselves from idols." The word "guard" means to garrison ourselves against attacks from without, like the assaults of the heresies. "Idols" refers to the heretical substitutes, brought in by the Gnostics and Cerinthians, for the true God, as revealed in this Epistle and in John's Gospel and referred to in the preceding verse. Idols here also refer to anything that replaces the real God. We as genuine children of the genuine God should be on the alert to guard ourselves from these heretical substitutes and all vain replacements of our genuine and real God, with whom we are organically one and who is eternal life to us. This is the aged apostle's word of warning to all his little children as a conclusion of his Epistle.

According to John's understanding, an idol is anything that replaces, is a substitute for, the subjective God, the God whom we have experienced and whom we are still experiencing. Through this enlightenment, we are able to understand 5:18-21 in a very experiential way.

John's last word, in 5:21, is the charge to guard ourselves from idols. Anything that is a substitute or replacement for the true God and eternal life is an idol. We need to live, walk, and have our being in this God and in this life. (*Life-study of 1 John,* pp. 356-357)

Further Reading: Life-study of 1 John, msgs. 39-40

Enlightenment and inspiration: _____

_____

_____

_____

Morning Nourishment

Isa.   **You are My witnesses, declares Jehovah, and My ser-**
43:10-11   **vant whom I have chosen, in order that you may**
know and believe Me and understand that I am He.
Before Me there was no God formed, neither will
there be any after Me. I, even I, am Jehovah; and there
is no Savior besides Me.

Before we were saved, we were outside of God. God was true in
Himself, but we could not say in our experience that He was true
to us. But after we believed in the Lord Jesus, we entered into
God. Therefore, 1 John 5:20 says not only that we know the true
One but also that we are in the true One....To be in the true One
[is to be]...in His Son Jesus Christ. Because we are in God, He
now experientially becomes true to us. Likewise,...Jesus Christ
...becomes experientially true to us. Due to our experience of God
and Christ by being in God and in Christ, we can say that this is
the true God and eternal life. (*Life-study of 1 John,* p. 356)

Today's Reading

John concludes 1 John 5:20:..."This is the true God and eternal
life." This...is not merely the conclusion of verse 20; it is actually
the conclusion of the entire book. What this Epistle reveals is the
true God and eternal life....If we do not live in the true God and eternal life, then we shall have a substitute for the true God, and this
substitute will be an idol. (*Life-study of 1 John,* pp. 356-357)

How could such a wonderful people [as Israel], who were God's
elect, God's vine, God's bride, God's flock, and God's treasure, become
rebels, briars and thorns, a harlot, scorpions, and dross?...The first
reason for their degradation was their idolatry. Ezekiel speaks
again and again about the idols among the people of Israel. We
should not consider that an idol is always an outward image. Idols
are substitutes for God. Ezekiel 14:3 says, "Son of man, these men
have set up their idols in their hearts." Those who set up idols in
their hearts are estranged from the Lord through their idols (v. 5).

Anything within us that is a substitute for God is an idol.
Whatever we love more than the Lord is an idol. A scholarship,

education, money, clothing, a wife, a husband, children—all these can be idols, something or someone that we love more than God and that replaces God in our life. Whatever is more important to us than the Lord is an idol. The first reason for the fall and degradation of Israel was idolatry.

In Revelation 2 we see that the degradation of the churches began with the leaving of the first love to the Lord (v. 4)....If we do not love the Lord with the first love, this is a sign that we have some kind of idol. Whatever we love more than the Lord is our idol. If we realize this, we will see that the cause of the degradation of Israel and of the church is exactly the same.

The people of Israel worshipped idols as substitutes for God. The situation is the same with a great many Christians today. Most Christians have lost their first love. Some love their missionary work much more than they love the Lord Himself. Others love their study of the Bible or their evangelistic outreach more than the Lord. Many care for their work, but they do not care for the Lord. Dr. A. W. Tozer of the Christian and Missionary Alliance once said that if the Lord Jesus came into a conference of Christian leaders, they would not recognize Him....Tozer's observation indicates that it is common for Christians to love many things other than the Lord Himself. (*Life-study of Ezekiel,* pp. 143-145)

Isaiah 43:10 and 11 say, "You are My witnesses, declares Jehovah, / And My servant whom I have chosen, / In order that you may know and believe Me / And understand that I am He. / Before Me there was no God formed, / Neither will there be any after Me. / I, even I, am Jehovah; / And there is no Savior besides Me." How can it be proved that only Jehovah is God? This can be proved only by a group of people who are God's witnesses. Those who are God's witnesses are also His servants. Christ is God's Witness and His Servant. Today, we, the church people, are one with Christ as God's witnesses and servants. (*Life-study of Isaiah,* pp. 153-154)

Further Reading: Life-study of Isaiah, msg. 49; *Life-study of Ezekiel,* msg. 13

Enlightenment and inspiration: _____

_____

_____

Hymns, #437

1   Hast thou heard Him, seen Him, known Him?
      Is not thine a captured heart?
    Chief among ten thousand own Him;
      Joyful choose the better part.

        Captivated by His beauty,
        Worthy tribute haste to bring;
        Let His peerless worth constrain thee,
        Crown Him now unrivaled King.

2   Idols once they won thee, charmed thee,
      Lovely things of time and sense;
    Gilded thus does sin disarm thee,
      Honeyed lest thou turn thee thence.

3   What has stripped the seeming beauty
      From the idols of the earth?
    Not a sense of right or duty,
      But the sight of peerless worth.

4   Not the crushing of those idols,
      With its bitter void and smart;
    But the beaming of His beauty,
      The unveiling of His heart.

5   Who extinguishes their taper
      Till they hail the rising sun?
    Who discards the garb of winter
      Till the summer has begun?

6   'Tis that look that melted Peter,
      'Tis that face that Stephen saw,
    'Tis that heart that wept with Mary,
      Can alone from idols draw:

7   Draw and win and fill completely,
      Till the cup o'erflow the brim;
    What have we to do with idols
      Who have companied with Him?

Composition for prophecy with main point and sub-points: _____

The All-inclusive Christ
in His Four Stages according to
God's New Testament Economy (1)—
In the Stage of His Incarnation

Scripture Reading: Isa. 52:14—53:3; 1 Cor. 1:22-24; 2 Cor. 8:9; Mark 6:1-6

Day 1 I. **The purpose of God's move in the stage of His incarnation is:**
  A. To bring God into man (Matt. 1:20-21, 23; Isa. 7:14; 9:6).
  B. To make God man that man may become God in life and nature but not in the Godhead (John 1:1, 14; 12:24).
  C. To mingle God with man that God and man may be one (Lev. 2:4-5).
  D. To accomplish God's redemption for man (Rom. 8:3; 1 Pet. 1:18-20; Heb. 9:26, 28, 12; 2:14).
  E. To carry out God's salvation in man (1 Tim. 1:15).
  F. To impart the divine life into man (1 John 4:9).

Day 2 II. **The incarnated Savior is the arm of Jehovah;**
&   **the arm of Jehovah is God Himself in His sav-**
Day 3 **ing power (Isa. 53:1b):**
  A. When the Lord Jesus came out to preach the gospel, that was the unveiling of the arm of Jehovah (Luke 4:14, 18-19; Mark 1:14-15).
  B. The Old Testament term is *the arm of Jehovah;* the New Testament term is *the power of God* (1 Cor. 1:24).
  C. Although Christ was unveiled as the arm of Jehovah, many did not see that He was Jehovah Himself coming in power to save them; they did not believe, because He grew up like a tender plant before Jehovah and like a root out of dry ground (Isa. 53:2a; John 1:46; Matt. 13:55).
  D. When the Lord Jesus comes back, the remnant of Israel will repent and wail and be saved (Zech. 12:10-14; Rom. 11:26-27); at that time they will

confess the contents of Isaiah 53, and this chapter
will be full of taste to them.

III. **As the complete God, signified by the arm of
Jehovah, the power of God, Christ became a
perfect man, signified by a man of sorrows
(vv. 1b, 3a; John 1:1, 14; 1 Tim. 2:5):**

A. The arm of Jehovah is Jehovah in His power, and
the man of sorrows is Jesus; when these two are
added together, they equal incarnation.

B. In 1 Corinthians 1:22-24 *Christ crucified* corresponds to the *man of sorrows* in Isaiah 53:3, and
the *power of God* corresponds to the *arm of Jehovah* in verse 1.

IV. **As a perfect man, the Lord Jesus lived a lowly
and sorrowful human life (vv. 2-3):**

A. He grew up like a tender plant before Jehovah
and like a root out of dry ground (v. 2a):

1. The plant here refers to a sprout, which is
tender, small, and delicate; because He was
such a small, delicate person, no one would
pay attention to Him.

2. He grew up like a root out of dry ground,
which signifies a difficult environment; this
means that He was born of a poor family
(v. 2a; Luke 2:21-24; cf. Lev. 12:8; 2 Cor. 8:9).

3. The Lord Jesus was raised in the home of a
poor carpenter in the despised town of Nazareth and in the despised region, Galilee; this
was the fulfillment of the dry ground in Isaiah
53:2a.

Day 4

4. The Lord's environment being one of dry ground
means that His environment did not render
Him any help at all:

a. Everything that He had was from God; He
did not receive or expect anything from
His surroundings that would encourage,
support, or comfort Him.

b. Our Lord had God's will as His satisfaction

all His life; He was satisfied only with God (John 4:34; 5:30; 6:38).

   c. Our Lord was never discouraged (Isa. 42:4; 49:4); He had no hope toward the world and did not expect to receive anything from it; His only hope was in God, and His only satisfaction was in God.

   d. Those who take their satisfaction in God will never be disappointed (John 4:13-14).

Day 5

B. He had no attracting form nor majesty that men should look upon Him (Isa. 53:2b):

  1. Jesus had neither an attracting form, nor did He have a beautiful appearance; He did not have any form or comeliness that would cause others to appreciate Him.

  2. Instead of majesty, Jesus had poverty (Matt. 8:20), and instead of an attractive form and a beautiful appearance, He had a visage and form that were marred (Isa. 52:14).

  3. *Visage* denotes the appearance and also refers to the face or facial expression; Christ's face and His form were marred (disfigured) in order that He might save us; this is astonishing, different from what people expected Christ as a servant of God to be (v. 15).

C. Christ was despised and forsaken of men, like one from whom men hide their faces and whom men do not esteem (53:3).

D. The Lord Jesus lived as a man of sorrows and acquainted with grief; this was a part of Christ's qualifications for accomplishing redemption (v. 3a).

E. He was a "man whose chief distinction was, that His life was one of constant painful endurance" (Keil and Delitzsch).

F. Christ's being such a man and His living such a lowly and sorrowful human life fully qualified Him to be the Redeemer and the Savior to save us from Satan, sin, death, and self (Heb. 2:14-18; Matt. 1:21; Rom. 8:3; 2 Tim. 1:10; Matt. 16:24-25).

Day 6   **V. Mark 6:1-6 may be regarded as a fulfillment of the prophecy in Isaiah 53:2-3:**

A. The Nazarenes, blinded by their natural knowledge, knew the Lord Jesus according to the flesh, not according to the Spirit (Mark 6:2-3; 2 Cor. 5:16).

B. Only in the Gospel of Mark is the Lord Jesus called a carpenter (6:3):

1. Carpentry is not a magnificent work, but it requires much fineness and patience; in such a work the Lord Jesus was found in fashion as a man (Phil. 2:8), not in loftiness but in lowliness, fineness, and patience.

2. In Mark 6:3 the word *carpenter* is used in a despising manner:

a. The Nazarenes were astounded by the Lord's teaching, by His wisdom, and by His works of power, but they regarded Him as a person of low status (vv. 2-3).

b. They were stumbled in Him because, although they heard wonderful words out of His mouth and saw some of His marvelous deeds, they considered that He did not have a high status or degree.

c. They saw the Lord Jesus as one who was merely a carpenter; therefore, they were stumbled in Him, and they despised Him.

C. The record in Mark 6:1-6 should cause us to ask ourselves what we want and what we value.

Morning Nourishment

Rom. ...God, sending His own Son in the likeness of the flesh
8:3 of sin and concerning sin, condemned sin in the flesh.
1 John In this the love of God was manifested among us, that
4:9 God sent His only begotten Son into the world that
we might have life and live through Him.
15 Whoever confesses that Jesus is the Son of God, God
abides in him and he in God.

The purpose of the incarnation is to bring God into man. God is
in us (1 John 4:15), and we have to realize that the first step God
took to get into us was to be incarnated. Furthermore, God was
incarnated not only in Jesus but also in us. To be saved is to have
God incarnated in you. This is because incarnation brings God
into man. Before you were saved, you had nothing to do with God.
But since the day you believed into the Lord Jesus, God was incarnated in you. This means that God came into you. In human history, God never came into man until four thousand years after His
creation of man. He was born into man to bring God into man.
When God comes into a person through regeneration, the incarnation is repeated again.

God in eternity past was God only, but in incarnation He was
made man. He made Himself man that man may become God in
life and in nature but not in the Godhead....We have been born of
God, and we are the sons of God....Since we are born of God, we
may say and even we should say that we are God in life and
nature but not in the Godhead. (*The Move of God in Man*, p. 26)

Today's Reading

The purpose of the incarnation is also to mingle God with man
that God and man may be one....We and God are one by being
mingled together.

The meal offering in Leviticus 2:4 is made of fine flour mingled
with oil. Two elements are mingled together to be one entity but
without a third element being produced. The English word *mingled* means that two elements are combined together but that
they remain distinguishable in their elements. The meal offering

is of two elements, the element of oil and the element of fine flour. No third element is produced. The truth of mingling can also be seen in 1 Corinthians 6:17, which says that "he who is joined to the Lord is one spirit." This indicates the mingling of the Lord as the Spirit with our spirit. The divine Spirit dwells in our human spirit, and these two mingle together as one spirit.

Another purpose of the incarnation was to accomplish God's redemption for man (Rom. 8:3; 1 Pet. 1:18-20; Heb. 9:26, 28, 12; 2:14). God cannot apply His redemptive work to us without being one with us. He died a vicarious death for us so that His death could now become our death (Gal. 2:20a). The only way this could be realized is by mingling. God is mingled with us, so now He is one with us. When He died on the cross, we died there with Him. Without our union with Him and without being joined to Him, His substitutionary death could not be applied to us. When we become one with Christ, whatever He has accomplished as our Substitute becomes ours.

The incarnation was also for the purpose of carrying out God's salvation in man (1 Tim. 1:15). We need not only God's redemption but also God's salvation. Redemption mostly deals with the negative things, and salvation is mostly to supply us with the positive things. For God to be our salvation, He needs to be one with us. Since He is one with us, His death was a vicarious death for our redemption. Also, His being everything to us as our life and nature means that He is our salvation. In order to be our salvation, He has to become one with us.

God was incarnated to impart the divine life into man. First John 4:9 says that "God sent His only begotten Son into the world that we might have life and live through Him." God came to be a man so that we could have His divine life. If He had never been a man, He could not come into us and we could not have Him as our divine life. Incarnation was for the impartation of the divine life into us. (*The Move of God in Man,* pp. 27-29)

Further Reading: The Move of God in Man, ch. 2

Enlightenment and inspiration: _____

_____
_____
_____

Morning Nourishment

Isa. Who has believed our report? And to whom has the
53:1-3 arm of Jehovah been revealed? For He grew up like a
tender plant before Him, and like a root out of dry
ground...He was despised and forsaken of men, a
man of sorrows...

1 Cor. ...We preach Christ crucified, to Jews a stumbling
1:23-24 block, and to Gentiles foolishness, but to those who
are called, both Jews and Greeks, Christ the power of
God and the wisdom of God.

The first stage of Christ, the stage of incarnation, was not a
part of His redemption. Christ is our Savior, and He did redeem
us, but His incarnation by itself was not His redemption. Isaiah
53:2 says, "For He grew up like a tender plant before Him, / And
like a root out of dry ground." Christ's being like a tender plant
and a root out of dry ground was not part of His redemption. Likewise, His not being esteemed (v. 3) was not part of His redemption.

Isaiah 53:1b-3 refers to Christ's incarnation....*The arm of
Jehovah* [v. 1] is a figure of speech signifying Jehovah Himself
in His power. Thus, the arm of Jehovah is God Himself in His
saving power. This arm of Jehovah has been revealed. Two thousand years ago, when the Lord Jesus came out of Nazareth to
preach the gospel, that was the unveiling of the arm of Jehovah.
Christ as the arm of Jehovah was revealed to many, but they did
not realize that He was the arm of Jehovah. They did not see that
He was Jehovah Himself coming in power to save them. (*Life-
study of Isaiah*, p. 389)

Today's Reading

Based on this revelation of the arm of Jehovah, the apostles
reported (1 John 1:3). But who has believed their report? When
the Lord Jesus comes back, the remnant of Israel will all repent
and wail. At that time they will recount Isaiah 53:1: "Who has
believed our report? / And to whom has the arm of Jehovah been
revealed?" Then they will go on to recount, "For..." The word *for* at

the beginning of verse 2 is a great word. Why did no one believe the report and receive the revelation concerning Christ? Because He grew up not like a king but like a tender plant before Jehovah. Because of this they did not believe the apostles' report. A number of times in the four Gospels the Jews despised the Lord Jesus, speaking words such as, "Can anything good be from Nazareth?" (John 1:46) and "Is not this the carpenter's son?" (Matt. 13:55). If Jesus had come out of Bethlehem, out of the city of the royal family, perhaps many Jews would believe in Him. But they have not believed, because He grew up like a tender plant before Jehovah, and like a root out of dry ground.

Isaiah 53:3 begins, "He was despised and forsaken of men, / A man of sorrows and acquainted with grief." In verse 1 Christ is referred to as the arm of Jehovah, and in verse 3 He is called a man of sorrows. The arm of Jehovah is Jehovah in His power, and the man of sorrows is Jesus. When these two are put together, they equal incarnation. One day Jehovah, the very Elohim, became a man by the name of Jesus. In Isaiah 53 Jehovah is signified by the arm of Jehovah, and Jesus is called a man of sorrows. This is incarnation.

As the complete God, signified by the arm of Jehovah, the power of God (v. 1b; 1 Cor. 1:24), Christ became a perfect man, signified by a man of sorrows (Isa. 53:3a; John 1:1, 14; 1 Tim. 2:5b). The Old Testament term is *the arm of Jehovah,* whereas the New Testament term is *the power of God.* First Corinthians 1:22-24 says, "For indeed Jews require signs and Greeks seek wisdom, but we preach Christ crucified, to Jews a stumbling block, and to Gentiles foolishness, but to those who are called, both Jews and Greeks, Christ the power of God and the wisdom of God." In these verses Christ crucified corresponds to the man of sorrows in Isaiah 53:3, and the power of God equals the arm of Jehovah in Isaiah 53:1. Thus, in these two portions of the Word, incarnation is clearly mentioned. (*Life-study of Isaiah,* pp. 389-390)

Further Reading: Life-study of Isaiah, msg. 50

Enlightenment and inspiration: _____

Morning Nourishment

Isa. He has no *attracting* form nor majesty that we should
53:2-3 look upon Him, nor beautiful appearance that we
should desire Him. He was despised and forsaken of
men, a man of sorrows and acquainted with grief;
and like one from whom *men* hide their faces, He was
despised; and we did not esteem Him.

As a perfect man, Christ lived a lowly and sorrowful human
life. His birth was lowly, and His family also was in a lowly state.
His living was also full of sorrow.

First, He grew up like a tender plant (like a small, delicate person) before Jehovah (Isa. 53:2a). The plant here actually refers to
a sprout, which is very tender, small, and delicate. Christ did not
grow up like a large tree, but like a small, delicate sprout. Because
He was such, no one would pay any attention to Him. He also
grew up like a root out of dry ground, meaning that He was born
of a poor family. His mother, Mary, and her husband, Joseph, lived
in a despised city called Nazareth, in a despised region, Galilee. It
is true that they were descendants of David, but David reigned
approximately one thousand years before Jesus was born. When
Mary and Joseph came into being, the royal family had become
insignificant. In Isaiah 11:1 the royal family of Jesse was likened
to the stump of a tree. From that stump a sprout, Christ, came
out. Hence, His birth was very lowly. (*Life-study of Isaiah*, p. 391)

Today's Reading

Second, the Lord Jesus had no attracting form nor majesty
that men should look upon Him, nor beautiful appearance that
men should desire Him (Isa. 53:2b). If Jesus had been very handsome and attractive, very majestic and powerful, everyone would
have been attracted to Him. But Jesus had neither an attracting
form nor majesty, nor did He have a beautiful appearance. Instead
of majesty, He had poverty, and instead of a beautiful appearance,
He had a visage and form that were disfigured (52:14).

Third, Christ was despised and forsaken of men, like one from
whom men hide their faces and whom men do not esteem (53:3).

Often when the Jews saw Him, they hid their faces. When He was hanging on the cross, many hid their faces from Him. Furthermore, they did not regard or respect Him. This was Christ's human living.

Fourth, Christ lived as a man of sorrows and acquainted with grief (53:3a). As a man in His human living, Christ did not have riches; rather, He had sorrows. Moreover, He was acquainted with grief. He knew nothing but sorrow and grief. This was not for redemption; rather, this was part of Christ's qualifications for accomplishing redemption.

Christ's being such a man and living such a lowly and sorrowful human life fully qualified Him to be the Savior to save fallen men from four things: Satan, sin, death, and self (Heb. 2:14-18; Matt. 1:21). All the foregoing items have nothing to do directly with redemption or salvation. These are only the qualifications that qualified Christ to be our Redeemer and our Savior.

Isaiah 53:1 concerns the revelation and report of Christ as the arm of Jehovah, the dynamic Redeemer....Here the word *arm* signifies the dynamic might of Christ in His divinity.

Verses 2 and 3 go on to speak regarding Christ's lowly birth and suffering in His humanity....In the Bible plants often typify humanity. For Christ to grow up like a tender plant before Jehovah means that Christ grew up before Him in His humanity. In His divinity Christ has always been perfect and complete, and thus there was no need for Him to grow in His divinity. His growth took place in His humanity. First He was a child, and then He grew into boyhood and eventually into manhood. Having become perfected and completed in His humanity, at the age of thirty He came forth to minister for God.

Verse 2 also tells us that, in His humanity, Christ had no attracting form nor majesty; He did not have a beautiful appearance. (*Life-study of Isaiah,* pp. 391-392, 181-182)

Further Reading: Life-study of Isaiah, msg. 27; *The Conclusion of the New Testament,* msg. 27

Enlightenment and inspiration: _____

_____

_____

_____

Morning Nourishment

Isa. He will not faint, nor will He be discouraged, until He
42:4 has established justice in the earth...
49:4 But I said, I have labored in vain; I have used up my
       strength for nothing and vanity; yet surely the justice
       due to me is with Jehovah, and my recompense with
       my God.

Isaiah 53:2 is a word concerning the Lord Jesus which I treasure very much: "For He grew up like a tender plant before Him, /
And like a root out of dry ground." What does this mean? In a
place where there is water, trees grow easily and quickly. However, the Lord's environment was such that it did not render Him
any help at all. His surroundings did not give Him anything. The
world did not help Him at all....Neither did...the angels give Him
any help. Everything He had was from God; He did not receive
anything from His surroundings that would encourage, support,
or comfort Him. His life was a straight line....Our Lord took the
straight path from this world to His destiny. He said that no one
who puts his hand on the plow and looks behind is fit for the kingdom of God. What does this mean? Those who have their hands
on the plow must look forward; otherwise, the furrows will be
crooked. When the eyes look forward, the plow will run straight. If
a person looks behind him, the furrow he plows will not be
straight. God does not want us to turn or to circle around. He is our
satisfaction. (*The Collected Works of Watchman Nee*, vol. 17, p. 190)

Today's Reading

Our Lord was never discouraged. What He experienced and
encountered in His environment during His lifetime should have
given Him much discouragement and disappointment. But He was
not discouraged or disappointed. Isaiah 49 says something concerning the Lord. It says that God intends for Christ to bring Jacob
back again to Him and gather Israel back again to Himself. But
outwardly everything seemed to have failed completely. How did
He feel? It says, "I have labored in vain; / I have used up my strength
for nothing and vanity; / Yet surely the justice due to me is with

Jehovah, / And my recompense with my God" (v. 4). He was not disappointed. Isaiah 42 also says that the Lord did not faint and was not discouraged. Although what He encountered could have caused Him to faint and be discouraged, He did not behave that way.

The emphasis of the Gospel of John is different from that of the Gospel of Matthew. The Lord in the Gospel of John was rejected by men from the beginning. The Lord in the Gospel of Matthew was not rejected until after chapter twelve. John 1 records that the Lord came to His own, and His own received Him not. He came to bear the sins of the people of Israel and the Gentiles. Yet men did not want Him; they rejected Him and would not receive Him. When He was on the cross, men rejected Him, and God also rejected Him. We would have been disappointed, discouraged, saddened, and grieved. But John 19 records that the Lord cried on the cross, "It is finished!" We would have cried, "It is over!" But He was shouting like a victorious army, "It is finished!" Throughout His life, He took satisfaction in God. He had no hope toward the world and did not expect to receive anything from it. His only hope was in God, and His only satisfaction was in God. He said that no one knows the Son except the Father, that He did not receive glory from men, that He did not come to do His own will but the will of the One who sent Him, and that He always did the will of the One who sent Him. Our Lord had God's will as His satisfaction all His life. He was satisfied only with God. This is why He was not disappointed no matter how people, events, and things in this world changed. Those who take their satisfaction in God will never be disappointed.

On the negative side, we should not cherish any hope concerning the world. If we do not expect any fame, glory, help, comfort, or support from this world, we will never be thirsty. We should take care of the way we view the water of this world. Our view concerning the world will surely determine our hope toward those in the world. (*The Collected Works of Watchman Nee,* vol. 17, pp. 183-184)

Further Reading: The Collected Works of Watchman Nee, vol. 17, pp. 181-190

Enlightenment and inspiration: _____
_____
_____
_____

Morning Nourishment

Isa. **Even as many were astonished at Him—His visage**
52:14-15 **was marred more than that of any man, and His form**
more than that of the sons of men—so will He sur-
prise many nations; kings will shut their mouths
because of Him; for what had not been recounted to
them they will see, and what they had not heard of
they will contemplate.

[Isaiah 52:14 says] that many will be astonished at Him: "Even
as many were astonished at Him—/ His visage was marred more
than that of any man, / And His form more than that of the sons of
men." The Hebrew word for *mar* here means to disfigure. The
word *visage* denotes the appearance and also refers to the face or
facial expression, the countenance. This was Isaiah's poetic writing. In such a poetic writing Isaiah portrayed Christ in the New
Testament sense. He was exalted and lifted up and is very high,
and He has acted prudently and has prospered in every way.
Today even the opposers of Christ respect Him. They all know
that Christ is a great One. But when we meet Him, we will see
that His face was marred, or disfigured. Christ was disfigured for
us. (*Life-study of Isaiah,* p. 367)

Today's Reading

On the one hand, Christ is now glorified, but on the other
hand, He still bears the impress of His being disfigured for us.
Today the Jews might know Christ somewhat as the glorious
Christ, but they do not know the disfigured Christ. We believers
know the disfigured Christ much more than the glorified Christ.
We were saved not only by a glorified Christ but also by a disfigured Christ. A so-called picture of Jesus popular among Christians today portrays Him as a handsome man. However, Christ
our Savior was not that handsome; rather, He was disfigured. Isaiah said that many people were astonished at this.

According to people's concept, Jesus is great, high, stately, and
glorified. Who would think that Jesus would be such a disfigured
One? After I preached the gospel in China, many learned ones,

after listening to the message, came to me and said, "Is this Jesus? We thought that Jesus Christ was a great man, a great figure. Is this disfigured One, this marred One, really Jesus?" Yes, this is Jesus. If He were not so, He could never save us; He could never be our Substitute on the cross. This is something astonishing.

Christ is exalted and lifted up and very high, but when men saw Him, He was different from what they expected Him to be. Hence, many were astonished at Him because His visage was marred, or disfigured, and His form also was marred. In your thought, in your imagination, what kind of Jesus do you have? In Christianity there is a so-called picture of Jesus, portraying Him as a very handsome man. However, we might be astonished to see that instead of being handsome, the Lord was disfigured. (*Life-study of Isaiah,* pp. 367, 375)

The word of the blind despisers here may be considered a fulfillment of the prophecy concerning the Slave-Savior in Isaiah 53:2 and 3: "Like a root out of dry ground. / He has no attracting form nor majesty that we should look upon Him, / Nor beautiful appearance that we should desire Him. / He was despised and forsaken of men." This was to know Him according to the flesh in His humanity, not according to the Spirit in His deity (Rom. 1:4). In His humanity He was a root out of dry ground, a sprout out of the stump of Jesse, and a branch out of his roots (Isa. 11:1), a Shoot unto David (Jer. 23:5; 33:15), the Shoot who was a man and the Servant of Jehovah (Zech. 3:8; 6:12), out of the seed of David according to the flesh (Rom. 1:3). In His deity He was the Shoot of Jehovah for beauty and glory (Isa. 4:2), the Son of God marked out in power according to the Spirit (Rom. 1:4). (*Life-study of Mark,* pp. 163-164)

The Hebrew word translated *sorrows* in Isaiah 53:3-4 literally means pains, either physical or mental. According to Keil and Delitzsch, Christ was a "man whose chief distinction was, that His life was one of constant painful endurance." He, as a man of sorrows, was a despised person. (*Life-study of Isaiah,* p. 182)

Further Reading: Life-study of Isaiah, msgs. 48-49

Enlightenment and inspiration: _____

_____
_____
_____

Morning Nourishment

Mark
6:1-4

And He...came into His own country...And when the Sabbath had come, He began to teach in the synagogue; and many hearing were astounded, saying, Where *did* this man *get* these things?...Is not this the carpenter?...And they were stumbled because of Him. And Jesus said to them, A prophet is not without honor except in his *own* country and among his *own* relatives and in his *own* house.

In Mark 6:1-6 the Lord was despised and rejected by the Nazarenes. Actually, this rejection did not disturb Him or disappoint Him. Even though He left them because of their rejection of Him, this does not mean that He was disappointed or that He gave them up. The Slave-Savior wanted to do something for the Nazarenes, but they would not open to Him. Mark 6:5 says, "And He could not do any work of power there, except to lay His hands upon a few of the sick and heal them." The unbelief of the Nazarenes kept the Lord from doing many works of power among them.

Instead of being discouraged and disappointed by the rejection of the Nazarenes, the Lord was encouraged. This is proved by the fact that in 6:7-13 He sent out the twelve to do the same thing He was doing. In particular, "He...gave them authority over the unclean spirits" (v. 7). The Lord appointed the twelve to do what He was doing. (*Life-study of Mark*, pp. 161-162)

Today's Reading

Immediately after the Lord did the wonderful work of bringing in the blessings of the kingdom, He came to His own country [Mark 6:1]....Verses 2 and 3 indicate that He was despised and rejected by the Nazarenes: "And when the Sabbath had come, He began to teach in the synagogue; and many hearing were astounded, saying, Where did this man get these things? And what is this wisdom given to this man, and how is it that such works of power take place through His hands? Is not this the carpenter, the son of Mary, and brother of James and Joses and Judas and Simon? And are not His sisters here with us? And they were stumbled

because of Him." Here we see that the Nazarenes knew
Savior according to the flesh, not according to the Spi
5:16). They were blinded by their natural knowledge.

The Lord Jesus then said to them, "A prophet is not ‚without
honor except in his own country and among his own relatives and
in his own house" (Mark 6:4). This word indicates that probably
even some of the Lord's own household joined in with the others
to despise and reject Him.

Only in the Gospel of Mark is the Lord Jesus called a carpenter. Those who rejected Him asked, "Is not this the carpenter?"
They used the word "carpenter" in a despising manner. They were
astounded by His teaching, by His wisdom, and by His works of
power. But they regarded Him as a person of low status. In today's
terms, they might have wondered what qualifications He had,
what kind of degree He had.

The word "stumbled" in 6:3 indicates that the Nazarenes
rejected the Slave-Savior. Why were they stumbled in Him? They
were stumbled in Him because, on the one hand, they heard wonderful words out of His mouth and saw some of His marvelous
deeds, and yet, on the other hand, they considered that He did not
have a high status or degree. They saw Him as one who was
merely a carpenter. Therefore, they were stumbled in Him, and
they despised Him.

The record in chapter six should cause us to ask ourselves what
we want and what we value. Do we want an advanced degree or a
high social status? In the Lord's recovery we want Jesus, and we
want the riches of Christ. Instead of the mere superficial doc-
trines in the Bible, we want the depths of the divine truths in the
Word of God. We would like to follow the Lord Jesus in ministering the riches of the Triune God to people and in presenting to
them the depths of the divine truth in the holy Scriptures. This is
what we want, and this is what we desire to do. (*Life-study of
Mark*, pp. 163-165)

Further Reading: Life-study of Mark, msg. 18

Enlightenment and inspiration: _____

Hymns, #86

1 Though Thou art God, most glorious, high,
Thou in the flesh to us came nigh,
A lowly man become thereby;
Lord, I remember Thee!

2 Glory divine was put away
Under the tent of flesh to stay,
No outward beauty to display;
Lord, I remember Thee!

3 Thou art a root from out dry ground,
Thou wast the Man of sorrows found,
Hated, despised by man around;
Lord, I remember Thee!

4 Gentle and lowly is Thy heart,
Willing to suffer all Thou art,
To God and man complaining not;
Lord, I remember Thee!

5 Thou as a man art tender, sweet,
Balanced in every way, complete,
Meal-offering to the Father meet;
Lord, I remember Thee!

6 Doing the Father's will Thy prize,
Never accepting Satan's lies,
None like Thyself, so faithful, wise;
Lord, I remember Thee!

7 For Thine obedience to God's will,
Willing to suffer deathly ill,
E'en on the Cross my place to fill,
Lord, I remember Thee!

8 Therefore hath God exalted Thee,
Given Thee glory, majesty,
Heaven and earth will bow the knee;
O Lord, I worship Thee!

Composition for prophecy with main point and sub-points: _____

**The All-inclusive Christ
in His Four Stages according to
God's New Testament Economy (2)—
In the Stage of His Crucifixion**

Scripture Reading: Isa. 53:4-10a, 12b

Day 1 I. "Surely He has borne our sicknesses, / And carried our sorrows; / Yet we ourselves esteemed Him stricken, / Smitten of God and afflicted. / But He was wounded because of our transgressions; / He was crushed because of our iniquities; / The chastening for our peace was upon Him, / And by His stripes we have been healed" (Isa. 53:4-5):

A. In the report of the prophets and the revelation of Jehovah (v. 1), Christ is revealed as the crucified Redeemer, who sacrificed Himself for our trespasses (our sin) to accomplish Jehovah's eternal redemption (vv. 4-10a; Heb. 9:12) that the believers in Christ may be redeemed (forgiven of sins—Acts 10:43, justified—13:39, and reconciled to God—Rom. 5:10), resulting in the life union with Christ in His resurrection (Isa. 53:10b), the reality of which is the life-giving Spirit (John 11:25; 1 Cor. 15:45b; Rom. 8:11).

B. Sicknesses and sorrows, like transgressions and iniquities (Isa. 53:5), come from sin; hence, they too need Christ's redemption (Psa. 103:1-3):

1. All healings accomplished on fallen people are a result of the Lord's redemption; on the cross He took away our infirmities, bore our diseases, and accomplished full healing for us (Matt. 8:17).

2. However, in this age the application of this divine healing power can be only a foretaste to us; in the coming age we will experience the full taste (Heb. 6:5).

C. Christ bore our sicknesses at the time when He

was judged by God on the cross, in the hour when God put all our iniquities on Him (Isa. 53:6b; 1 Pet. 2:24).

Day 2   D. Christ's suffering of death healed our death so that we might live in His resurrection (v. 24).

E. The experience of the children of Israel at Marah portrays that as we experience the cross of Christ and live a crucified life, Christ's resurrection life becomes our healing power, and the Lord becomes our Healer (Exo. 15:22-26; 1 Pet. 2:24; Matt. 8:17; 9:12; Isa. 53:4-5; cf. 61:1):

1. Just as Moses saw a vision of a tree and cast this tree into the bitter waters, we need to see a vision of the crucified and resurrected Christ as the tree of life and apply Him to our bitter situations and our bitter being (Exo. 15:25-26):

   a. First Peter 2:24 indicates that this tree signifies the cross of Christ, or the crucified Christ; the cross is the tree, and the One who died on the tree is our Healer (Exo. 15:25-26; cf. Gal. 3:13).

   b. This tree also signifies the resurrected Christ because the tree was cast into the bitter waters of Marah after the children of Israel had traveled three days in the wilderness (Exo. 15:22).

   c. The tree of life in Revelation 2:7 signifies the crucified (implied in the tree as a piece of wood—1 Pet. 2:24) and resurrected (implied in the life of God—John 11:25) Christ.

2. The crucified and resurrected Christ is the tree of life, and this tree is Jehovah our Healer, the One who heals the bitterness of our circumstances and the bitterness of our being, turning this bitterness into the sweet waters of His inward presence (Rev. 2:7; Exo. 15:22-26; 1 Pet. 2:24-25).

Day 3

F. Through Christ's healing death and life-dispensing resurrection, He became the Shepherd and Overseer of our souls (vv. 24-25; Isa. 53:6; John 21:15-17).

II. **"We all like sheep have gone astray; / Each of us has turned to his own way, / And Jehovah has caused the iniquity of us all / To fall on Him" (Isa. 53:6):**

A. It was when God was judging Jesus on the cross that He caused the iniquity of us all to fall on Him, making Jesus, in the eyes of God, the unique sinner at that moment (Matt. 27:45-46; Psa. 22:1).

B. Christ's death was not merely a murder (Acts 7:52), nor was it a martyrdom; rather, it was carried out by God Himself according to His law.

C. Thus, Christ died a vicarious death as the Substitute for sinners (1 Pet. 3:18), a death that was legal according to God's law and was recognized and approved by God according to the law.

D. The flesh of the passover lamb, typifying the crucified Christ, was to be roasted with fire and was not to be eaten raw or boiled (Exo. 12:8-9):

1. To be roasted with fire signifies Christ's suffering under the holy fire of God's judgment (Isa. 53:4, 10; Psa. 22:14-15; John 19:28).

2. To be eaten raw signifies not to believe in Christ's redemption but to regard Him merely as an example of human life to be imitated.

3. To be eaten boiled signifies regarding His death on the cross not as death for redemption but as the suffering of human persecution for martyrdom.

Day 4

E. Just as the flesh of the passover lamb was to be eaten for life supply, so we need to eat Christ for our life supply (Exo. 12:8-10; John 6:53, 55-57; cf. Deut. 15:19-20):

1. To solve the problem of the fall of man and to accomplish God's original intention, both life and redemption are needed.

2. God's judicial redemption through the blood of Christ is the procedure to reach God's goal of dispensing Christ as life into us for our organic salvation (Rom. 5:10).

III. **"He was oppressed, and it was He who was afflicted, / Yet He did not open His mouth; / Like a lamb that is led to the slaughter / And like a sheep that is dumb before its shearers, / So He did not open His mouth. / By oppression and by judgment He was taken away; / And as for His generation, who among them had the thought / That He was cut off out of the land of the living / For the transgression of my people to whom the stroke was due?" (Isa. 53:7-8):**

A. In His vicarious death for sinners, Christ was oppressed, afflicted, and led to the slaughter like a lamb and sheared before the shearers like a sheep, with no reaction (Acts 8:32; Matt. 27:12-14).

B. Christ was oppressed by the hypocritical Jewish leaders (26:57, 59, 65-68) and then judged by the unjust Roman officials (Luke 23:1-12; John 18:33-38; 19:1-16); by these two things He was taken away and crucified.

Day 5

C. No one among Christ's generation understood that He was cut off out of the land of the living for the transgression of the prophet's people, the Jews, to whom the stroke was due.

IV. **"And they assigned His grave with the wicked, / But with a rich man in His death, / Although He had done no violence, / Nor was there any deceit in His mouth" (Isa. 53:9):**

A. Those who crucified Christ planned to bury Him with the two transgressors, the wicked ones (Luke 23:32-33), but eventually God in His sovereignty caused Christ to be buried in a rich man's tomb (Matt. 27:57-60).

B. The word for "death" in Isaiah 53:9 is plural in Hebrew, *deaths,* signifying "a violent death, the

very pain of which makes it like dying again and
again" (Keil and Delitzsch).

V. **"But Jehovah was pleased to crush Him, to
afflict Him with grief. / When He makes Himself an offering for sin" (v. 10a):**

A. Because Christ was crushed for our iniquities,
Satan can be crushed under our feet (Rom. 16:20),
and because He was afflicted with grief, we can be
filled with His joy (John 16:20-22).

B. Christ bore our sin in its totality, dying on the
cross to be the reality of the sin offering and the
trespass offering (1:29; cf. Heb. 10:5-10; 1 John
1:7-9; Lev. 4—5).

C. Christ's precious blood shed for the forgiveness of
our sins is also the blood of the covenant; because
of the blood of Jesus, we have boldness for entering the Holy of Holies, where we can enjoy God,
behold His beauty, and receive His infusion (Matt.
26:28; Heb. 10:19-20; cf. Lev. 16:11-16; Psa. 27:4).

Day 6   D. Christ came into the death waters, was wounded
by us and for our transgressions, and secretes His
life into us to make us precious pearls for the
building of God's eternal expression (Isa. 53:5;
Rev. 21:21; John 19:34).

VI. **"He poured out His life unto death / And was
numbered with the transgressors, / Yet He alone
bore the sin of many / And interceded for the
transgressors" (Isa. 53:12b):**

A. Man, God, and Christ all had a part in Christ's crucifixion; man did the murdering, the killing (Acts
7:52), but God carried out the legal judgment to kill
Christ as a legal Substitute so that Christ might
die a vicarious death for sinners (Isa. 53:6b, 10a).

B. Moreover, Christ Himself was willing to be such
an offering; He made Himself that offering (v. 10b),
and He poured out His life for that purpose (John
10:17-18; Heb. 9:14).

C. When Christ was crucified on the cross, He was
numbered with the transgressors, and He

interceded for the transgressors (Luke 23:32-34a; cf. Heb. 7:25):

1. He interceded for them regarding the evil of the transgressors, the result of their ignorance, a trespass that He prayed would be forgiven by God.

2. Stephen prayed for his persecutors in the same way that his Lord, whom he loved and lived, had prayed for His (Acts 7:60).

Morning Nourishment

Isa.   Surely He has borne our sicknesses, and carried our
53:4-5 sorrows; yet we ourselves esteemed Him stricken, smitten of God and afflicted. But He was wounded because
of our transgressions; He was crushed because of our
iniquities; the chastening for our peace was upon Him,
and by His stripes we have been healed.

In the report of the prophets [Isa. 53:1] and the revelation of
Jehovah [52:15], Christ was revealed as the crucified Redeemer.
As our Redeemer, Christ sacrificed Himself for our trespasses, or
for our sin, for the accomplishing of Jehovah's eternal redemption
(53:4-10a). It is difficult to understand how one who is great could
be crucified. Those who are crucified are usually very low and mean.
Nevertheless, our Redeemer was crucified, sacrificing Himself for
our trespasses for the accomplishing of God's eternal redemption.
(*Life-study of Isaiah,* pp. 378-379)

Today's Reading

Christ's crucifixion was for the accomplishing of God's eternal
redemption (Heb. 9:12), that the believers in Christ may be redeemed (forgiven of sins—Acts 10:43, justified—Acts 13:39, and
reconciled to God—Rom. 5:10) unto the life union in His resurrection, the reality of which is the life-giving Spirit (1 Cor. 15:45b;
Rom. 8:9b; Phil. 1:19b). Christ's redemption includes forgiveness
of sins, justification, and reconciliation to God. As sinners, we all
needed forgiveness and justification. We were not only sinners
but also enemies of God; thus, we also needed reconciliation.
Christ's redemption did all this for us.

Romans 5:18 says that justification is "of life." This means that
justification is for life, or unto life. We are justified that we may
have life. This life is a life union in Christ's resurrection....We enter
into this union by being redeemed. Through Christ's redemption,
we are justified unto this life union in His resurrection, the reality
of which is the life-giving Spirit.

Christ's death was a vicarious death (Isa. 53:4-10a, 12b)....He
died not for Himself but for us. He died in our place. Christ's death

was not a martyrdom; Christ was put to death by God for us (v. 4b). Thus, His death was a vicarious death.

In His vicarious death, Christ bore our sicknesses and carried our sorrows. "Surely He has borne our sicknesses, / And carried our sorrows; / Yet we ourselves esteemed Him stricken, / Smitten of God and afflicted. / But He was wounded because of our transgressions; / He was crushed because of our iniquities; / The chastening for our peace was upon Him, / And by His stripes we have been healed. / We all like sheep have gone astray; / Each of us has turned to his own way, / And Jehovah has caused the iniquity of us all / To fall on Him" (vv. 4-6). These verses use the words *sicknesses* and *sorrows* along with *transgressions* and *iniquities* (that is, sins). ...Sicknesses and sorrows are mentioned with transgressions and iniquities because our sicknesses and sorrows come from one thing—sin....Since our sicknesses and sorrows come from sin, they also need Christ's redemption....Christ bore our sicknesses and carried our sorrows in His vicarious death. (*Life-study of Isaiah,* pp. 400-401, 182-183)

All healings accomplished on fallen people are due to the Lord's redemption. He took our infirmities and bore our diseases on His cross [Matt. 8:17] and accomplished full healing for us there. However, the application of healing by divine power can only be a foretaste in this age; the full taste will be accomplished in the coming age. (*Life-study of Matthew,* p. 317)

In His vicarious death for us, the sinners, Christ bore our sicknesses and carried our sorrows (Isa. 53:4). It may seem that He did this while He was ministering on the earth, because at a time when He healed many sick ones, Matthew 8:17, quoting the word in Isaiah 53:4, says, "He Himself took away our infirmities and bore our diseases." Actually, Christ bore our sicknesses at the moment He was judged by God on the cross, in the hour when God put all our iniquities upon Him. (*Life-study of Isaiah,* pp. 392-393)

Further Reading: Life-study of Isaiah, msg. 27; *Life-study of Romans,* msg. 10

Enlightenment and inspiration: _____

_____

_____

_____

Morning Nourishment

1 Pet. **Who Himself bore up our sins in His body on the tree,**
2:24-25 **in order that we, having died to sins, might live to**
            righteousness; by whose bruise you were healed. For
            you were like sheep being led astray, but you have now
            returned to the Shepherd and Overseer of your souls.

First Peter 2:24...speaks of Christ as our Savior, our Redeemer....According to this verse, we have been healed by Christ's bruise. This is the healing of death. We were dead (Eph. 2:1), but Christ's suffering of death healed our death so that we may live in His resurrection. (*Life-study of 1 Peter,* p. 187)

Today's Reading

Just as the Lord tested the children of Israel at Marah [Exo. 15:22-27], He uses our experience of His cross in bitter circumstances to test us and to prove us. By testing us, He shows us where we are and what we are. He exposes our motives, intentions, and desires. Nothing tests us more than the experience of the cross....Through such an application of the cross, the Lord heals us. This kind of healing is very different from the so-called healings that take place in healing campaigns. I have attended such campaigns, and not once did I see a genuine healing. Real healing takes place as we receive the dealing of the cross....Then Christ's resurrection life becomes our healing power, and the Lord becomes our Healer.

As a true servant of the Lord, instead of striving with this murmuring and complaining people, Moses cried out to the Lord (v. 25). In response to his cry, the Lord showed him a tree (v. 25). When Moses cast the tree into the waters, the waters were made sweet. First Peter 2:24 indicates that this tree signifies the cross of Christ. Thus, the tree that healed the bitter waters denotes the cross on which the Lord was crucified. The cross of Christ, the unique cross, is the healing cross.

First Peter 2:24...indicates that the cross is the tree and that the One who died on the cross is our Healer. He was crucified for our healing. If we would experience His healing, we need to be identified with His crucifixion. (*Life-study of Exodus,* pp. 353-354, 350, 354)

   In Greek the word for *tree* in Revelation 2:7, as in 1 Peter 2:24, means *wood;* it is not the word usually used for *tree.* In the Bible the tree of life always signifies Christ as the embodiment of all the riches of God (Col. 2:9) for our food (Gen. 2:9; 3:22, 24; Rev. 22:2, 14, 19). In Revelation 2:7 it signifies the crucified (implied in the tree as a piece of wood—1 Pet. 2:24) and resurrected (implied in the life of God—John 11:25) Christ. (Rev. 2:7, footnote 6)

   As we walk in the realm of resurrection, we shall be led to Marah again and again. Every time we experience the healing tree cast into our circumstances, we spontaneously realize that something in our being needs to be healed. We may sense the need for healing in the mind, or realize that our will needs to be adjusted, or see that our emotion needs to be balanced. (*Life-study of Exodus,* p. 353)

   It is significant that the journey from the Red Sea to Marah was exactly three days. [The Israelites'] being three days in the wilderness in thirst means that they were buried for three days, that they were in death. The third day may be considered as the day of resurrection since the Lord Jesus was raised on the third day (1 Cor. 15:4). When the children of Israel came to the bitter waters of Marah on the third day, the Lord showed Moses a tree, and when Moses cast this tree into the waters, the waters became sweet (Exo. 15:25). We may say that the tree is the resurrected Christ because this tree was cast into the bitter waters of Marah after the children of Israel had traveled three days in the wilderness. (*The Crucial Revelation of Life in the Scriptures,* pp. 35-36)

   Christ was our Redeemer in His death on the tree (1 Pet. 2:24). Now He is our soul's Shepherd and Overseer in the resurrection life within us. As such, He is able to guide us and supply us with life that we may follow in His steps according to the model of His suffering (v. 21). (1 Pet. 2:25, footnote 2)

Further Reading: Life-study of Exodus, msg. 30; *The Crucial Revelation of Life in the Scriptures,* ch. 4

Enlightenment and inspiration: _____

_____

_____

_____

Morning Nourishment

Isa. 53:6 We all like sheep have gone astray; each of us has turned to his own way, and Jehovah has caused the iniquity of us all to fall on Him.

Exo. 12:9 Do not eat any of it raw or boiled at all with water, but roasted with fire—its head with its legs and with its inward parts.

It was man who oppressed Christ, afflicted Him, judged Him, led Him to the slaughter, put Him on the cross, and crucified Him between two transgressors. After man had done all these things, Jehovah caused the iniquity of us all, who have gone astray like sheep and have turned to our own way, to fall on Him (Isa. 53:6). In Isaiah 53:6, the phrase *us all* refers to the remnant of the Jews at the time of the Lord Jesus' coming back. At that time all the remaining Jews will repent and will speak the words of this verse. Jehovah caused the iniquity of us all to fall upon the man who was oppressed, judged, afflicted, and crucified. (*Life-study of Isaiah,* p. 396)

Today's Reading

God caused all the iniquity of His chosen people to fall upon Christ, taking Him as our Substitute, legally, according to God's law. God removed all the iniquities from us and put them on Christ, making Christ the unique sinner. Then God forsook Him because at that time He was our Substitute. Thus, Christ died a vicarious death, a death that was recognized and approved by God's law.

If a man dies while attempting to rescue someone who is drowning, that death can be considered a bold death but not a vicarious death. Something that is vicarious must be related to the law. The bold death of a rescuer is not a death that can be recognized by God's law. But Christ died a vicarious death that was legal according to God's law and was recognized by God. That death of Christ was recognized by God legally, according to His law, as the vicarious death of the One who was the Substitute for us, the sinners.

Christ's death was much more than a murder....Furthermore,

Christ's death was not a martyrdom. Christ was not killed by His enemies because of His philosophy or His teachings. Christ's death was something carried out by God Himself according to His law. Hence, His death was the death of One who was a Substitute for others; it was a vicarious death....Christ's death was not merely a murder, nor was it a martyrdom; rather, it was a death for the accomplishing of redemption, a redeeming death. We all need to know the truth concerning Christ's vicarious death. (*Life-study of Isaiah,* pp. 396-398)

In Exodus 12:8 the children of Israel were given the proper way to eat the flesh of the passover lamb: roasted with fire. Fire here signifies God's holy wrath exercised in judgment. When Christ was on the cross, the holy fire of God judged Him and consumed Him.

In 12:9 the children of Israel were charged not to eat of the lamb raw. Today those who do not believe in Christ's redemption attempt to eat Him "raw." This means that they regard Christ as a model or example of human living for them to imitate. In effect, to do this is to eat the passover lamb raw.

Furthermore, the children of Israel were not to eat the lamb boiled with water (12:9). To eat of Christ as if He were "boiled with water" is to regard His death on the cross not as death for redemption, but as martyrdom. Many today do not believe that Christ died as the Redeemer. According to their concept, He was persecuted by man and died as a martyr, having sacrificed Himself for His teachings. To apply Christ's death in this way is to eat the lamb boiled with water. To be boiled in water is to undergo suffering, but not the suffering of holy fire. Rather, this suffering is simply the suffering of persecution.

Christ suffered for us under God's judgment. He was burned and "roasted" by the holy fire of God's wrath. As our Redeemer, He was judged for us. (*Life-study of Exodus,* pp. 257-258)

Further Reading: Life-study of Exodus, msg. 23; The Crucial Revelation of Life in the Scriptures, ch. 3

Enlightenment and inspiration: _____

_____
_____
_____

Morning Nourishment

Rom. **For if we, being enemies, were reconciled to God**
5:10 **through the death of His Son, much more we will be**
       saved in His life, having been reconciled.
Isa. **He was oppressed, and it was He who was afflicted,**
53:7 **yet He did not open His mouth; like a lamb that is led**
       to the slaughter and like a sheep that is dumb before
       its shearers, so He did not open His mouth.

The flesh of the passover lamb was to be eaten for life supply
(Exo. 12:8-10). The same is true of the Lord Jesus as the fulfillment of the type. Each of the Gospels speaks of the blood of
Christ. The Gospel of John, however, goes on to say that the
flesh of Christ is edible. In John 6:53 the Lord Jesus says that
we must eat the flesh of the Son of Man, and in verse 55 He
declares, "My flesh is true food." Flesh here signifies the life of
Christ. The life of Christ is edible; it is our life supply. This is
mentioned in the Gospel of John because this Gospel…is focused
on life. Therefore, this Gospel reveals that the blood of Christ
redeems and that the life of Christ supplies. Hallelujah, we
have the blood of the Lamb for redemption and the flesh of the
Lamb for the supply of life! (*Life-study of Exodus,* p. 257)

Today's Reading

God's complete salvation is of two aspects: the judicial aspect
and the organic aspect.…Exodus 12 shows us the way to keep the
Passover.…Every household of the children of Israel had to kill a
lamb. Once the lamb was killed, it was divided into two parts, one
part being the blood and the other part, the flesh.

On the judicial side the blood was sprinkled on the door to
meet God's need; on the organic side the flesh was eaten and received
into the children of Israel to meet their need for moving on. The
way before them was quite long, at least three days' journey.…
Without eating the flesh of the lamb, they would be overtaken by
the Egyptians. Therefore, every household had to eat the flesh of
the lamb until they were full that they might be ready to take the
journey ahead. This is the organic side.

Hence, the Passover in the Old Testament shows us that God's salvation has the redeeming aspect and the saving aspect. The redeeming aspect, signified by the blood of the lamb, is according to God's judicial requirement; the saving aspect, signified by the flesh of the lamb, is according to God's organic provision of life. (*The Organic Aspect of God's Salvation,* pp. 19-21)

In His vicarious death for sinners, Christ was oppressed, afflicted, and led to the slaughter like a lamb and sheared before the shearers like a sheep, with no reaction (Isa. 53:7). First, Christ was oppressed; then He was afflicted. Affliction is more serious than oppression. Then, third, He was led to the slaughter.

On the night in which He was betrayed, He was praying in Gethsemane. Then the soldiers came and arrested Him and bound Him. That was an oppression. As a man, Christ was entitled to certain human rights. He had done nothing wrong. Therefore, for people to come and arrest Him was an oppression. After being arrested, He was judged, first by the Jewish leaders according to their religious law, and, second, by the Roman officials according to Roman law. While they were judging Him, people spat on Him and mocked Him. These were afflictions. After all this, they made the decision to crucify Him. Then they led Him like a lamb to the slaughter and like a sheep to be sheared before the shearers. Christ was not only led to the slaughter; He was even sheared like a sheep by the shearers, the Jewish people. Yet, He did not react against any of this. He did not argue, vindicate Himself, or justify Himself; instead, He was silent. This surprised Pilate (Matt. 27:13-14).

Isaiah 53:8 says that Christ was taken away by oppression (of the hypocritical Jewish leaders—Matt. 26:57, 59, 65-68) and by judgment (of the unjust Roman officials—Luke 23:1-12; John 18:33-38; 19:1-16). First, Christ was oppressed; then He was judged. By these two things He was taken away. All these things are included in and issued in His crucifixion. (*Life-study of Isaiah,* pp. 394-395)

Further Reading: The Organic Aspect of God's Salvation, chs. 1-2

Enlightenment and inspiration: _____
_____
_____
_____

Morning Nourishment

Isa. And they assigned His grave with the wicked, but with
53:9-10 a rich man in His death, although He had done no violence, nor was there any deceit in His mouth. But
Jehovah was pleased to crush Him, to afflict Him with
grief. When He makes Himself an offering for sin...
Heb. Having therefore, brothers, boldness for entering the
10:19 *Holy of* Holies in the blood of Jesus.

Isaiah 53:8b [says], "And as for His generation, who among
them had the thought / That He was cut off out of the land of the
living / For the transgression of my people to whom the stroke was
due?" This means that no one understood that it was for us that
Christ suffered persecution and judgment and died. Even those
who were with the Lord Jesus when He was dying on the cross
did not understand that He was dying for them. The stroke that
should have been the due of God's people fell on Him. He suffered
death for us. (*Life-study of Isaiah,* p. 184)

Today's Reading

According to Isaiah 53:9, Christ was assigned a grave with the
wicked, but with a rich man in His death, although He had done no
violence, nor was there any deceit in His mouth. Those who crucified Him planned to bury Him with the two transgressors, the
wicked ones; but eventually God in His sovereignty caused Christ
to be buried in a rich man's tomb. After Christ died, a rich man,
Joseph of Arimathea, came to claim His body, and he put the body
into a new tomb (Matt. 27:57-60). Christ had done no violence, nor
was there any deceit in His mouth, yet people treated Him in a
mean way. But God in His sovereignty came in to carry out His
justice. After Christ died, God's judgment had been completed, so
God immediately took Him away from any kind of suffering and
put Him in a rich man's tomb. (*Life-study of Isaiah,* pp. 395-396)

According to Isaiah 53:10a, in Christ's vicarious death as the
Substitute for sinners, Jehovah was pleased to crush Him, to
afflict Him with grief.

Isaiah 53:10b says that Christ made Himself an offering for

sin. This means that Christ volunteered to make Himself an offering for sin. In Hebrew the word translated *Himself* in this verse literally means "His soul." The composition of this verse can also have the sense of "When His soul would make an offering for sin." This implies that Christ volunteered to be an offering for sin. The offering here is not a sin offering but an offering for sin, referring to sin in its totality. Likewise, John 1:29, speaking of Christ as "the Lamb of God, who takes away the sin of the world," does not refer to the sin offering (although the sin offering is included there) but to an offering for sin in its totality—for wrongdoings, mistakes, trespasses, transgressions, evildoings, and iniquities. (*Life-study of Isaiah,* pp. 398-399)

The blood of the covenant is not mainly for forgiveness; it is primarily for God to be our portion. God has ordained and predestinated us to enjoy Him. This enjoyment has also been covenanted to us. What enacted this covenant? It was enacted by the blood of Jesus Christ, the blood which brings us into all the divine blessings.

In the New Testament we see that the Lord Jesus shed His blood on the cross. This is typified by the blood of the Passover lamb in Exodus 12. With the blood shed on the cross the Lord enacted the new testament. This is typified by the blood in Exodus 24. Ultimately, the blood of Christ brings us into the fullness of God as our eternal enjoyment. This aspect of the blood, the blood of the eternal covenant, is typified by the blood in Leviticus 16.

The blood brings us into the Holy of Holies; that is, it brings us into God. When the high priest entered into the Holy of Holies, it was not his purpose to observe the law. On the contrary, because of the blood sprinkled in the Holy of Holies, he could enjoy God, behold His beauty, and receive His infusion. Enjoying God in this way is what produces a man of God. (*Life-study of Exodus,* pp. 933-934)

Further Reading: Life-study of Isaiah, msg. 50; *Life-study of Exodus,* msg. 79

Enlightenment and inspiration: _____

_____
_____
_____

Morning Nourishment

John But one of the soldiers pierced His side with a spear,
19:34 and immediately there came out blood and water.
Isa. ...Because He poured out His life unto death and was
53:12 numbered with the transgressors, yet He alone bore
       the sin of many and interceded for the transgressors.
Luke And Jesus said, Father, forgive them, for they do not
23:34 know what they are doing....

Revelation 21:21 tells us that the twelve gates of the New Jerusalem are twelve pearls. A pearl is not created or manufactured but produced by an oyster...organically just as a piece of fruit is not something manufactured or created but is the produce of an organic tree. The fact that an oyster produces a pearl is quite significant. Pearls are produced by oysters in the waters of death. When the oyster is wounded by a particle of sand, a little rock, it secretes its life-juice around the sand and makes it a precious pearl.

In this allegory, we need to see the illustration of Christ's death. The oyster depicts Christ as the living One coming into the death waters, being wounded by us, and secreting His life over us to make us precious pearls for the building of God's eternal habitation and expression. (*God's New Testament Economy,* pp. 341-342)

Today's Reading

Isaiah 53:12b says that Christ poured out His life unto death. The Hebrew word for *life* literally means "soul." Thus, the Lord poured out His soul unto death. This corresponds with the Lord's word in John 10:17-18: "I lay down My life that I may take it again. No one takes it away from Me, but I lay it down of Myself. I have authority to lay it down, and I have authority to take it again. This commandment I received from My Father." In the Lord's death He laid down His life, and in His resurrection He received it back.

Christ poured out His human life to be an offering. Every offering, if it is a sacrifice, must be killed,...and the blood must be shed. Then it can be an offering accepted by God. In His death Christ poured out His life in such a way.

Thus far, we can see that in Christ's crucifixion, man did

something, God did something, and Christ Himself did something. Christ's crucifixion could not have been accomplished without the participation of any one of the three parties. Man did the murdering, the killing, but God carried out the legal judgment to kill Him as a legal Substitute that He might die a vicarious death for the ones for whom He died as a Substitute. Moreover, He Himself was willing to be such an offering. He made Himself that offering, and He poured out His life for that purpose.

According to Isaiah 53:12c, when Christ was crucified on the cross, He was numbered with the transgressors (Luke 23:32-33) and He interceded for the transgressors (v. 34a). Christ was crucified between two criminals....Thus, He was numbered with the transgressors....While on the cross, Christ interceded not only for His companions, the transgressors, who were beside Him, but also for those who were killing Him. He prayed for the transgressors. (*Life-study of Isaiah,* pp. 399-400, 395)

The fact that Christ was executed with two criminals indicates that the Roman authorities considered Him a criminal. This was done under God's sovereignty that the prophecy of Isaiah concerning Christ's execution might be fulfilled.

In Isaiah 53:12 it is prophesied that Christ would make intercession for the transgressors. According to Luke 23:34, the fulfillment of this prophecy, Jesus said, "Father, forgive them; for they do not know what they are doing." While He was on the cross the Lord made intercession for the transgressors, mainly for the Jews. He interceded for them regarding the evil of the transgressors, the result of their ignorance, a trespass that He prayed would be forgiven by God. (*The Conclusion of the New Testament,* pp. 386-387)

[In Acts 7:60] Stephen prayed for his persecutors in the same way that his Lord, whom he loved and lived, had prayed for His (Luke 23:34). (Acts 7:60, footnote 1)

Further Reading: God's New Testament Economy, msg. 33; *The Conclusion of the New Testament,* msgs. 36-37*

Enlightenment and inspiration: _____

_____
_____
_____

Hymns, #108

1   "Man of Sorrows," what a name
For the Son of God who came
Ruined sinners to reclaim!
    Hallelujah! what a Savior!

2   Bearing shame and scoffing rude,
In my place condemned He stood;
Sealed my pardon with His blood;
    Hallelujah! what a Savior!

3   Guilty, vile, and helpless, we,
Spotless Lamb of God was He;
Full redemption—can it be?
    Hallelujah! what a Savior!

4   Lifted up was He to die,
"It is finished!" was His cry;
Now in heaven exalted high;
    Hallelujah! what a Savior!

5   When He comes, our glorious King,
To His kingdom us to bring,
Then anew this song we'll sing:
    Hallelujah! what a Savior!

Composition for prophecy with main point and sub-points:

Reading Schedule for the Recovery Version of the Old Testament with Footnotes

Wk.	Lord's Day	Monday	Tuesday	Wednesday	Thursday	Friday	Saturday
1	☐ Gen 1:1-5	☐ 1:6-23	☐ 1:24-31	☐ 2:1-9	☐ 2:10-25	☐ 3:1-13	☐ 3:14-24
2	☐ 4:1-26	☐ 5:1-32	☐ 6:1-22	☐ 7:1—8:3	☐ 8:4-22	☐ 9:1-29	☐ 10:1-32
3	☐ 11:1-32	☐ 12:1-20	☐ 13:1-18	☐ 14:1-24	☐ 15:1-21	☐ 16:1-16	☐ 17:1-27
4	☐ 18:1-33	☐ 19:1-38	☐ 20:1-18	☐ 21:1-34	☐ 22:1-24	☐ 23:1—24:27	☐ 24:28-67
5	☐ 25:1-34	☐ 26:1-35	☐ 27:1-46	☐ 28:1-22	☐ 29:1-35	☐ 30:1-43	☐ 31:1-55
6	☐ 32:1-32	☐ 33:1—34:31	☐ 35:1-29	☐ 36:1-43	☐ 37:1-36	☐ 38:1—39:23	☐ 40:1—41:13
7	☐ 41:14-57	☐ 42:1-38	☐ 43:1-34	☐ 44:1-34	☐ 45:1-28	☐ 46:1-34	☐ 47:1-31
8	☐ 48:1-22	☐ 49:1-15	☐ 49:16-33	☐ 50:1-26	☐ Exo 1:1-22	☐ 2:1-25	☐ 3:1-22
9	☐ 4:1-31	☐ 5:1-23	☐ 6:1-30	☐ 7:1-25	☐ 8:1-32	☐ 9:1-35	☐ 10:1-29
10	☐ 11:1-10	☐ 12:1-14	☐ 12:15-36	☐ 12:37-51	☐ 13:1-22	☐ 14:1-31	☐ 15:1-27
11	☐ 16:1-36	☐ 17:1-16	☐ 18:1-27	☐ 19:1-25	☐ 20:1-26	☐ 21:1-36	☐ 22:1-31
12	☐ 23:1-33	☐ 24:1-18	☐ 25:1-22	☐ 25:23-40	☐ 26:1-14	☐ 26:15-37	☐ 27:1-21
13	☐ 28:1-21	☐ 28:22-43	☐ 29:1-21	☐ 29:22-46	☐ 30:1-10	☐ 30:11-38	☐ 31:1-17
14	☐ 31:18—32:35	☐ 33:1-23	☐ 34:1-35	☐ 35:1-35	☐ 36:1-38	☐ 37:1-29	☐ 38:1-31
15	☐ 39:1-43	☐ 40:1-38	☐ Lev 1:1-17	☐ 2:1-16	☐ 3:1-17	☐ 4:1-35	☐ 5:1-19
16	☐ 6:1-30	☐ 7:1-38	☐ 8:1-36	☐ 9:1-24	☐ 10:1-20	☐ 11:1-47	☐ 12:1-8
17	☐ 13:1-28	☐ 13:29-59	☐ 14:1-18	☐ 14:19-32	☐ 14:33-57	☐ 15:1-33	☐ 16:1-17
18	☐ 16:18-34	☐ 17:1-16	☐ 18:1-30	☐ 19:1-37	☐ 20:1-27	☐ 21:1-24	☐ 22:1-33
19	☐ 23:1-22	☐ 23:23-44	☐ 24:1-23	☐ 25:1-23	☐ 25:24-55	☐ 26:1-24	☐ 26:25-46
20	☐ 27:1-34	☐ Num 1:1-54	☐ 2:1-34	☐ 3:1-51	☐ 4:1-49	☐ 5:1-31	☐ 6:1-27
21	☐ 7:1-41	☐ 7:42-88	☐ 7:89—8:26	☐ 9:1-23	☐ 10:1-36	☐ 11:1-35	☐ 12:1—13:33
22	☐ 14:1-45	☐ 15:1-41	☐ 16:1-50	☐ 17:1—18:7	☐ 18:8-32	☐ 19:1-22	☐ 20:1-29
23	☐ 21:1-35	☐ 22:1-41	☐ 23:1-30	☐ 24:1-25	☐ 25:1-18	☐ 26:1-65	☐ 27:1-23
24	☐ 28:1-31	☐ 29:1-40	☐ 30:1—31:24	☐ 31:25-54	☐ 32:1-42	☐ 33:1-56	☐ 34:1-29
25	☐ 35:1-34	☐ 36:1-13	☐ Deut 1:1-46	☐ 2:1-37	☐ 3:1-29	☐ 4:1-49	☐ 5:1-33
26	☐ 6:1—7:26	☐ 8:1-20	☐ 9:1-29	☐ 10:1-22	☐ 11:1-32	☐ 12:1-32	☐ 13:1—14:21

Reading Schedule for the Recovery Version of the Old Testament with Footnotes

Wk.	Lord's Day	Monday	Tuesday	Wednesday	Thursday	Friday	Saturday
27	☐ 14:22—15:23	☐ 16:1-22	☐ 17:1—18:8	☐ 18:9—19:21	☐ 20:1—21:17	☐ 21:18—22:30	☐ 23:1-25
28	☐ 24:1-22	☐ 25:1-19	☐ 26:1-19	☐ 27:1-26	☐ 28:1-68	☐ 29:1-29	☐ 30:1—31:29
29	☐ 31:30—32:52	☐ 33:1-29	☐ 34:1-12	☐ Josh 1:1-18	☐ 2:1-24	☐ 3:1-17	☐ 4:1-24
30	☐ 5:1-15	☐ 6:1-27	☐ 7:1-26	☐ 8:1-35	☐ 9:1-27	☐ 10:1-43	☐ 11:1—12:24
31	☐ 13:1-33	☐ 14:1—15:63	☐ 16:1—18:28	☐ 19:1-51	☐ 20:1—21:45	☐ 22:1-34	☐ 23:1—24:33
32	☐ Judg 1:1-36	☐ 2:1-23	☐ 3:1-31	☐ 4:1-24	☐ 5:1-31	☐ 6:1-40	☐ 7:1-25
33	☐ 8:1-35	☐ 9:1-57	☐ 10:1—11:40	☐ 12:1—13:25	☐ 14:1—15:20	☐ 16:1-31	☐ 17:1—18:31
34	☐ 19:1-30	☐ 20:1-48	☐ 21:1-25	☐ Ruth 1:1-22	☐ 2:1-23	☐ 3:1-18	☐ 4:1-22
35	☐ 1 Sam 1:1-28	☐ 2:1-36	☐ 3:1—4:22	☐ 5:1—6:21	☐ 7:1—8:22	☐ 9:1-27	☐ 10:1—11:15
36	☐ 12:1—13:23	☐ 14:1-52	☐ 15:1-35	☐ 16:1-23	☐ 17:1-58	☐ 18:1-30	☐ 19:1-24
37	☐ 20:1-42	☐ 21:1—22:23	☐ 23:1—24:22	☐ 25:1-44	☐ 26:1-25	☐ 27:1—28:25	☐ 29:1—30:31
38	☐ 31:1-13	☐ 2 Sam 1:1-27	☐ 2:1-32	☐ 3:1-39	☐ 4:1—5:25	☐ 6:1-23	☐ 7:1-29
39	☐ 8:1—9:13	☐ 10:1—11:27	☐ 12:1-31	☐ 13:1-39	☐ 14:1-33	☐ 15:1—16:23	☐ 17:1—18:33
40	☐ 19:1-43	☐ 20:1—21:22	☐ 22:1-51	☐ 23:1-39	☐ 24:1-25	☐ 1 Kings 1:1-19	☐ 1:20-53
41	☐ 2:1-46	☐ 3:1-28	☐ 4:1-34	☐ 5:1—6:38	☐ 7:1-22	☐ 7:23-51	☐ 8:1-36
42	☐ 8:37-66	☐ 9:1-28	☐ 10:1-29	☐ 11:1-43	☐ 12:1-33	☐ 13:1-34	☐ 14:1-31
43	☐ 15:1-34	☐ 16:1—17:24	☐ 18:1-46	☐ 19:1-21	☐ 20:1-43	☐ 21:1—22:53	☐ 2 Kings 1:1-18
44	☐ 2:1—3:27	☐ 4:1-44	☐ 5:1—6:33	☐ 7:1-20	☐ 8:1-29	☐ 9:1-37	☐ 10:1-36
45	☐ 11:1—12:21	☐ 13:1—14:29	☐ 15:1-38	☐ 16:1-20	☐ 17:1-41	☐ 18:1-37	☐ 19:1-37
46	☐ 20:1—21:26	☐ 22:1-20	☐ 23:1-37	☐ 24:1—25:30	☐ 1 Chron 1:1-54	☐ 2:1—3:24	☐ 4:1—5:26
47	☐ 6:1-81	☐ 7:1-40	☐ 8:1-40	☐ 9:1-44	☐ 10:1—11:47	☐ 12:1-40	☐ 13:1—14:17
48	☐ 15:1—16:43	☐ 17:1-27	☐ 18:1—19:19	☐ 20:1—21:30	☐ 22:1—23:32	☐ 24:1—25:31	☐ 26:1-32
49	☐ 27:1-34	☐ 28:1—29:30	☐ 2 Chron 1:1-17	☐ 2:1—3:17	☐ 4:1—5:14	☐ 6:1-42	☐ 7:1—8:18
50	☐ 9:1—10:19	☐ 11:1—12:16	☐ 13:1—15:19	☐ 16:1—17:19	☐ 18:1—19:11	☐ 20:1-37	☐ 21:1—22:12
51	☐ 23:1—24:27	☐ 25:1—26:23	☐ 27:1—28:27	☐ 29:1-36	☐ 30:1—31:21	☐ 32:1-33	☐ 33:1—34:33
52	☐ 35:1—36:23	☐ Ezra 1:1-11	☐ 2:1-70	☐ 3:1—4:24	☐ 5:1—6:22	☐ 7:1-28	☐ 8:1-36

Reading Schedule for the Recovery Version of the Old Testament with Footnotes

Wk.	Lord's Day	Monday	Tuesday	Wednesday	Thursday	Friday	Saturday
53	☐ 9:1—10:44	☐ Neh 1:1-11	☐ 2:1—3:32	☐ 4:1—5:19	☐ 6:1-19	☐ 7:1-73	☐ 8:1-18
54	☐ 9:1-20	☐ 9:21-38	☐ 10:1—11:36	☐ 12:1-47	☐ 13:1-31	☐ Esth 1:1-22	☐ 2:1—3:15
55	☐ 4:1—5:14	☐ 6:1—7:10	☐ 8:1-17	☐ 9:1—10:3	☐ Job 1:1-22	☐ 2:1—3:26	☐ 4:1—5:27
56	☐ 6:1—7:21	☐ 8:1—9:35	☐ 10:1—11:20	☐ 12:1—13:28	☐ 14:1—15:35	☐ 16:1—17:16	☐ 18:1—19:29
57	☐ 20:1—21:34	☐ 22:1—23:17	☐ 24:1—25:6	☐ 26:1—27:23	☐ 28:1—29:25	☐ 30:1—31:40	☐ 32:1—33:33
58	☐ 34:1—35:16	☐ 36:1-33	☐ 37:1-24	☐ 38:1-41	☐ 39:1-30	☐ 40:1-24	☐ 41:1-34
59	☐ 42:1-17	☐ Psa 1:1-6	☐ 2:1—3:8	☐ 4:1—6:10	☐ 7:1—8:9	☐ 9:1—10:18	☐ 11:1—15:5
60	☐ 16:1—17:15	☐ 18:1-50	☐ 19:1—21:13	☐ 22:1-31	☐ 23:1—24:10	☐ 25:1—27:14	☐ 28:1—30:12
61	☐ 31:1—32:11	☐ 33:1—34:22	☐ 35:1—36:12	☐ 37:1-40	☐ 38:1—39:13	☐ 40:1—41:13	☐ 42:1—43:5
62	☐ 44:1-26	☐ 45:1-17	☐ 46:1—48:14	☐ 49:1—50:23	☐ 51:1—52:9	☐ 53:1—55:23	☐ 56:1—58:11
63	☐ 59:1—61:8	☐ 62:1—64:10	☐ 65:1—67:7	☐ 68:1-35	☐ 69:1—70:5	☐ 71:1—72:20	☐ 73:1—74:23
64	☐ 75:1—77:20	☐ 78:1-72	☐ 79:1—81:16	☐ 82:1—84:12	☐ 85:1—87:7	☐ 88:1—89:52	☐ 90:1—91:16
65	☐ 92:1—94:23	☐ 95:1—97:12	☐ 98:1—101:8	☐ 102:1—103:22	☐ 104:1—105:45	☐ 106:1-48	☐ 107:1-43
66	☐ 108:1—109:31	☐ 110:1—112:10	☐ 113:1—115:18	☐ 116:1—118:29	☐ 119:1-32	☐ 119:33-72	☐ 119:73-120
67	☐ 119:121-176	☐ 120:1—124:8	☐ 125:1—128:6	☐ 129:1—132:18	☐ 133:1—135:21	☐ 136:1—138:8	☐ 139:1—140:13
68	☐ 141:1—144:15	☐ 145:1—147:20	☐ 148:1—150:6	☐ Prov 1:1-33	☐ 2:1—3:35	☐ 4:1—5:23	☐ 6:1-35
69	☐ 7:1—8:36	☐ 9:1—10:32	☐ 11:1—12:28	☐ 13:1—14:35	☐ 15:1-33	☐ 16:1-33	☐ 17:1-28
70	☐ 18:1-24	☐ 19:1—20:30	☐ 21:1—22:29	☐ 23:1-35	☐ 24:1—25:28	☐ 26:1—27:27	☐ 28:1—29:27
71	☐ 30:1-33	☐ 31:1-31	☐ Eccl 1:1-18	☐ 2:1—3:22	☐ 4:1—5:20	☐ 6:1—7:29	☐ 8:1—9:18
72	☐ 10:1—11:10	☐ 12:1-14	☐ S.S 1:1-8	☐ 1:9-17	☐ 2:1-17	☐ 3:1-11	☐ 4:1-8
73	☐ 4:9-16	☐ 5:1-16	☐ 6:1-13	☐ 7:1-13	☐ 8:1-14	☐ Isa 1:1-11	☐ 1:12-31
74	☐ 2:1-22	☐ 3:1-26	☐ 4:1-6	☐ 5:1-30	☐ 6:1-13	☐ 7:1-25	☐ 8:1-22
75	☐ 9:1-21	☐ 10:1-34	☐ 11:1—12:6	☐ 13:1-22	☐ 14:1-14	☐ 14:15-32	☐ 15:1—16:14
76	☐ 17:1—18:7	☐ 19:1-25	☐ 20:1—21:17	☐ 22:1-25	☐ 23:1-18	☐ 24:1-23	☐ 25:1-12
77	☐ 26:1-:21	☐ 27:1-13	☐ 28:1-29	☐ 29:1-24	☐ 30:1-33	☐ 31:1—32:20	☐ 33:1-24
78	☐ 34:1-17	☐ 35:1-10	☐ 36:1-22	☐ 37:1-38	☐ 38:1—39:8	☐ 40:1-31	☐ 41:1-29

Reading Schedule for the Recovery Version of the Old Testament with Footnotes

Wk.	Lord's Day	Monday	Tuesday	Wednesday	Thursday	Friday	Saturday
79	42:1-25	43:1-28	44:1-28	45:1-25	46:1-13	47:1-15	48:1-22
80	49:1-13	49:14-26	50:1—51:23	52:1-15	53:1-12	54:1-17	55:1-13
81	56:1-12	57:1-21	58:1-14	59:1-21	60:1-22	61:1-11	62:1-12
82	63:1-19	64:1-12	65:1-25	66:1-24	Jer 1:1-19	2:1-19	2:20-37
83	3:1-25	4:1-31	5:1-31	6:1-30	7:1-34	8:1-22	9:1-26
84	10:1-25	11:1—12:17	13:1-27	14:1-22	15:1-21	16:1—17:27	18:1-23
85	19:1—20:18	21:1—22:30	23:1-40	24:1—25:38	26:1—27:22	28:1—29:32	30:1-24
86	31:1-23	31:24-40	32:1-44	33:1-26	34:1-22	35:1-19	36:1-32
87	37:1-21	38:1-28	39:1—40:16	41:1—42:22	43:1—44:30	45:1—46:28	47:1—48:16
88	48:17-47	49:1-22	49:23-39	50:1-27	50:28-46	51:1-27	51:28-64
89	52:1-34	Lam 1:1-22	2:1-22	3:1-39	3:40-66	4:1-22	5:1-22
90	Ezek 1:1-14	1:15-28	2:1—3:27	4:1—5:17	6:1—7:27	8:1—9:11	10:1—11:25
91	12:1—13:23	14:1—15:8	16:1-63	17:1—18:32	19:1-14	20:1-49	21:1-32
92	22:1-31	23:1-49	24:1-27	25:1—26:21	27:1-36	28:1-26	29:1—30:26
93	31:1—32:32	33:1-33	34:1-31	35:1—36:21	36:22-38	37:1-28	38:1—39:29
94	40:1-27	40:28-49	41:1-26	42:1—43:27	44:1-31	45:1-25	46:1-24
95	47:1-23	48:1-35	Dan 1:1-21	2:1-30	2:31-49	3:1-30	4:1-37
96	5:1-31	6:1-28	7:1-12	7:13-28	8:1-27	9:1-27	10:1-21
97	11:1-22	11:23-45	12:1-13	Hosea 1:1-11	2:1-23	3:1—4:19	5:1-15
98	6:1-11	7:1-16	8:1-14	9:1-17	10:1-15	11:1-12	12:1-14
99	13:1—14:9	Joel 1:1-20	2:1-16	2:17-32	3:1-21	Amos 1:1-15	2:1-16
100	3:1-15	4:1—5:27	6:1—7:17	8:1—9:15	Obad 1-21	Jonah 1:1-17	2:1—4:11
101	Micah 1:1-16	2:1—3:12	4:1—5:15	6:1—7:20	Nahum 1:1-15	2:1—3:19	Hab 1:1-17
102	2:1-20	3:1-19	Zeph 1:1-18	2:1-15	3:1-20	Hag 1:1-15	2:1-23
103	Zech 1:1-21	2:1-13	3:1-10	4:1-14	5:1—6:15	7:1—8:23	9:1-17
104	10:1—11:17	12:1—13:9	14:1-21	Mal 1:1-14	2:1-17	3:1-18	4:1-6

Reading Schedule for the Recovery Version of the New Testament with Footnotes

Wk.	Lord's Day	Monday	Tuesday	Wednesday	Thursday	Friday	Saturday
1	☐ Matt 1:1-2	☐ 1:3-7	☐ 1:8-17	☐ 1:18-25	☐ 2:1-23	☐ 3:1-6	☐ 3:7-17
2	☐ 4:1-11	☐ 4:12-25	☐ 5:1-4	☐ 5:5-12	☐ 5:13-20	☐ 5:21-26	☐ 5:27-48
3	☐ 6:1-8	☐ 6:9-18	☐ 6:19-34	☐ 7:1-12	☐ 7:13-29	☐ 8:1-13	☐ 8:14-22
4	☐ 8:23-34	☐ 9:1-13	☐ 9:14-17	☐ 9:18-34	☐ 9:35—10:5	☐ 10:6-25	☐ 10:26-42
5	☐ 11:1-15	☐ 11:16-30	☐ 12:1-14	☐ 12:15-32	☐ 12:33-42	☐ 12:43—13:2	☐ 13:3-12
6	☐ 13:13-30	☐ 13:31-43	☐ 13:44-58	☐ 14:1-13	☐ 14:14-21	☐ 14:22-36	☐ 15:1-20
7	☐ 15:21-31	☐ 15:32-39	☐ 16:1-12	☐ 16:13-20	☐ 16:21-28	☐ 17:1-13	☐ 17:14-27
8	☐ 18:1-14	☐ 18:15-22	☐ 18:23-35	☐ 19:1-15	☐ 19:16-30	☐ 20:1-16	☐ 20:17-34
9	☐ 21:1-11	☐ 21:12-22	☐ 21:23-32	☐ 21:33-46	☐ 22:1-22	☐ 22:23-33	☐ 22:34-46
10	☐ 23:1-12	☐ 23:13-39	☐ 24:1-14	☐ 24:15-31	☐ 24:32-51	☐ 25:1-13	☐ 25:14-30
11	☐ 25:31-46	☐ 26:1-16	☐ 26:17-35	☐ 26:36-46	☐ 26:47-64	☐ 26:65-75	☐ 27:1-26
12	☐ 27:27-44	☐ 27:45-56	☐ 27:57—28:15	☐ 28:16-20	☐ Mark 1:1	☐ 1:2-6	☐ 1:7-13
13	☐ 1:14-28	☐ 1:29-45	☐ 2:1-12	☐ 2:13-28	☐ 3:1-19	☐ 3:20-35	☐ 4:1-25
14	☐ 4:26-41	☐ 5:1-20	☐ 5:21-43	☐ 6:1-29	☐ 6:30-56	☐ 7:1-23	☐ 7:24-37
15	☐ 8:1-26	☐ 8:27—9:1	☐ 9:2-29	☐ 9:30-50	☐ 10:1-16	☐ 10:17-34	☐ 10:35-52
16	☐ 11:1-16	☐ 11:17-33	☐ 12:1-27	☐ 12:28-44	☐ 13:1-13	☐ 13:14-37	☐ 14:1-26
17	☐ 14:27-52	☐ 14:53-72	☐ 15:1-15	☐ 15:16-47	☐ 16:1-8	☐ 16:9-20	☐ Luke 1:1-4
18	☐ 1:5-25	☐ 1:26-46	☐ 1:47-56	☐ 1:57-80	☐ 2:1-8	☐ 2:9-20	☐ 2:21-39
19	☐ 2:40-52	☐ 3:1-20	☐ 3:21-38	☐ 4:1-13	☐ 4:14-30	☐ 4:31-44	☐ 5:1-26
20	☐ 5:27—6:16	☐ 6:17-38	☐ 6:39-49	☐ 7:1-17	☐ 7:18-23	☐ 7:24-35	☐ 7:36-50
21	☐ 8:1-15	☐ 8:16-25	☐ 8:26-39	☐ 8:40-56	☐ 9:1-17	☐ 9:18-26	☐ 9:27-36
22	☐ 9:37-50	☐ 9:51-62	☐ 10:1-11	☐ 10:12-24	☐ 10:25-37	☐ 10:38-42	☐ 11:1-13
23	☐ 11:14-26	☐ 11:27-36	☐ 11:37-54	☐ 12:1-12	☐ 12:13-21	☐ 12:22-34	☐ 12:35-48
24	☐ 12:49-59	☐ 13:1-9	☐ 13:10-17	☐ 13:18-30	☐ 13:31—14:6	☐ 14:7-14	☐ 14:15-24
25	☐ 14:25-35	☐ 15:1-10	☐ 15:11-21	☐ 15:22-32	☐ 16:1-13	☐ 16:14-22	☐ 16:23-31
26	☐ 17:1-19	☐ 17:20-37	☐ 18:1-14	☐ 18:15-30	☐ 18:31-43	☐ 19:1-10	☐ 19:11-27

Reading Schedule for the Recovery Version of the New Testament with Footnotes

Wk.	Lord's Day	Monday	Tuesday	Wednesday	Thursday	Friday	Saturday
27	☐ Luke 19:28-48	☐ 20:1-19	☐ 20:20-38	☐ 20:39—21:4	☐ 21:5-27	☐ 21:28-38	☐ 22:1-20
28	☐ 22:21-38	☐ 22:39-54	☐ 22:55-71	☐ 23:1-43	☐ 23:44-56	☐ 24:1-12	☐ 24:13-35
29	☐ 24:36-53	☐ John 1:1-13	☐ 1:14-18	☐ 1:19-34	☐ 1:35-51	☐ 2:1-11	☐ 2:12-22
30	☐ 2:23—3:13	☐ 3:14-21	☐ 3:22-36	☐ 4:1-14	☐ 4:15-26	☐ 4:27-42	☐ 4:43-54
31	☐ 5:1-16	☐ 5:17-30	☐ 5:31-47	☐ 6:1-15	☐ 6:16-31	☐ 6:32-51	☐ 6:52-71
32	☐ 7:1-9	☐ 7:10-24	☐ 7:25-36	☐ 7:37-52	☐ 7:53—8:11	☐ 8:12-27	☐ 8:28-44
33	☐ 8:45-59	☐ 9:1-13	☐ 9:14-34	☐ 9:35—10:9	☐ 10:10-30	☐ 10:31—11:4	☐ 11:5-22
34	☐ 11:23-40	☐ 11:41-57	☐ 12:1-11	☐ 12:12-24	☐ 12:25-36	☐ 12:37-50	☐ 13:1-11
35	☐ 13:12-30	☐ 13:31-38	☐ 14:1-6	☐ 14:7-20	☐ 14:21-31	☐ 15:1-11	☐ 15:12-27
36	☐ 16:1-15	☐ 16:16-33	☐ 17:1-5	☐ 17:6-13	☐ 17:14-24	☐ 17:25—18:11	☐ 18:12-27
37	☐ 18:28-40	☐ 19:1-16	☐ 19:17-30	☐ 19:31-42	☐ 20:1-13	☐ 20:14-18	☐ 20:19-22
38	☐ 20:23-31	☐ 21:1-14	☐ 21:15-22	☐ 21:23-25	☐ Acts 1:1-8	☐ 1:9-14	☐ 1:15-26
39	☐ 2:1-13	☐ 2:14-21	☐ 2:22-36	☐ 2:37-41	☐ 2:42-47	☐ 3:1-18	☐ 3:19—4:22
40	☐ 4:23-37	☐ 5:1-16	☐ 5:17-32	☐ 5:33-42	☐ 6:1—7:1	☐ 7:2-29	☐ 7:30-60
41	☐ 8:1-13	☐ 8:14-25	☐ 8:26-40	☐ 9:1-19	☐ 9:20-43	☐ 10:1-16	☐ 10:17-33
42	☐ 10:34-48	☐ 11:1-18	☐ 11:19-30	☐ 12:1-25	☐ 13:1-12	☐ 13:13-43	☐ 13:44—14:5
43	☐ 14:6-28	☐ 15:1-12	☐ 15:13-34	☐ 15:35—16:5	☐ 16:6-18	☐ 16:19-40	☐ 17:1-18
44	☐ 17:19-34	☐ 18:1-17	☐ 18:18-28	☐ 19:1-20	☐ 19:21-41	☐ 20:1-12	☐ 20:13-38
45	☐ 21:1-14	☐ 21:15-26	☐ 21:27-40	☐ 22:1-21	☐ 22:22-29	☐ 22:30—23:11	☐ 23:12-15
46	☐ 23:16-30	☐ 23:31—24:21	☐ 24:22—25:5	☐ 25:6-27	☐ 26:1-13	☐ 26:14-32	☐ 27:1-26
47	☐ 27:27—28:10	☐ 28:11-22	☐ 28:23-31	☐ Rom 1:1-2	☐ 1:3-7	☐ 1:8-17	☐ 1:18-25
48	☐ 1:26—2:10	☐ 2:11-29	☐ 3:1-20	☐ 3:21-31	☐ 4:1-12	☐ 4:13-25	☐ 5:1-11
49	☐ 5:12-17	☐ 5:18—6:5	☐ 6:6-11	☐ 6:12-23	☐ 7:1-12	☐ 7:13-25	☐ 8:1-2
50	☐ 8:3-6	☐ 8:7-13	☐ 8:14-25	☐ 8:26-39	☐ 9:1-18	☐ 9:19—10:3	☐ 10:4-15
51	☐ 10:16—11:10	☐ 11:11-22	☐ 11:23-36	☐ 12:1-3	☐ 12:4-21	☐ 13:1-14	☐ 14:1-12
52	☐ 14:13-23	☐ 15:1-13	☐ 15:14-33	☐ 16:1-5	☐ 16:6-24	☐ 16:25-27	☐ 1 Cor 1:1-4

Reading Schedule for the Recovery Version of the New Testament with Footnotes

Wk.	Lord's Day	Monday	Tuesday	Wednesday	Thursday	Friday	Saturday
53	1 Cor 1:5-9 ☐	1:10-17 ☐	1:18-31 ☐	2:1-5 ☐	2:6-10 ☐	2:11-16 ☐	3:1-9
54	3:10-13 ☐	3:14-23 ☐	4:1-9 ☐	4:10-21 ☐	5:1-13 ☐	6:1-11 ☐	6:12-20
55	7:1-16 ☐	7:17-24 ☐	7:25-40 ☐	8:1-13 ☐	9:1-15 ☐	9:16-27 ☐	10:1-4
56	10:5-13 ☐	10:14-33 ☐	11:1-6 ☐	11:7-16 ☐	11:17-26 ☐	11:27-34 ☐	12:1-11
57	12:12-22 ☐	12:23-31 ☐	13:1-13 ☐	14:1-12 ☐	14:13-25 ☐	14:26-33 ☐	14:34-40
58	15:1-19 ☐	15:20-28 ☐	15:29-34 ☐	15:35-49 ☐	15:50-58 ☐	16:1-9 ☐	16:10-24
59	2 Cor 1:1-4 ☐	1:5-14 ☐	1:15-22 ☐	1:23—2:11 ☐	2:12-17 ☐	3:1-6 ☐	3:7-11
60	3:12-18 ☐	4:1-6 ☐	4:7-12 ☐	4:13-18 ☐	5:1-8 ☐	5:9-15 ☐	5:16-21
61	6:1-13 ☐	6:14—7:4 ☐	7:5-16 ☐	8:1-15 ☐	8:16-24 ☐	9:1-15 ☐	10:1-6
62	10:7-18 ☐	11:1-15 ☐	11:16-33 ☐	12:1-10 ☐	12:11-21 ☐	13:1-10 ☐	13:11-14
63	Gal 1:1-5 ☐	1:6-14 ☐	1:15-24 ☐	2:1-13 ☐	2:14-21 ☐	3:1-4 ☐	3:5-14
64	3:15-22 ☐	3:23-29 ☐	4:1-7 ☐	4:8-20 ☐	4:21-31 ☐	5:1-12 ☐	5:13-21
65	5:22-26 ☐	6:1-10 ☐	6:11-15 ☐	6:16-18 ☐	Eph 1:1-3 ☐	1:4-6 ☐	1:7-10
66	1:11-14 ☐	1:15-18 ☐	1:19-23 ☐	2:1-5 ☐	2:6-10 ☐	2:11-14 ☐	2:15-18
67	2:19-22 ☐	3:1-7 ☐	3:8-13 ☐	3:14-18 ☐	3:19-21 ☐	4:1-4 ☐	4:5-10
68	4:11-16 ☐	4:17-24 ☐	4:25-32 ☐	5:1-10 ☐	5:11-21 ☐	5:22-26 ☐	5:27-33
69	6:1-9 ☐	6:10-14 ☐	6:15-18 ☐	6:19-24 ☐	Phil 1:1-7 ☐	1:8-18 ☐	1:19-26
70	1:27—2:4 ☐	2:5-11 ☐	2:12-16 ☐	2:17-30 ☐	3:1-6` ☐	3:7-11 ☐	3:12-16
71	3:17-21 ☐	4:1-9 ☐	4:10-23 ☐	Col 1:1-8 ☐	1:9-13 ☐	1:14-23 ☐	1:24-29
72	2:1-7 ☐	2:8-15 ☐	2:16-23 ☐	3:1-4 ☐	3:5-15 ☐	3:16-25 ☐	4:1-18
73	1 Thes 1:1-3 ☐	1:4-10 ☐	2:1-12 ☐	2:13—3:5 ☐	3:6-13 ☐	4:1-10 ☐	4:11—5:11
74	5:12-28 ☐	2 Thes 1:1-12 ☐	2:1-17 ☐	3:1-18 ☐	1 Tim 1:1-2 ☐	1:3-4 ☐	1:5-14
75	1:15-20 ☐	2:1-7 ☐	2:8-15 ☐	3:1-13 ☐	3:14—4:5 ☐	4:6-16 ☐	5:1-25
76	6:1-10 ☐	6:11-21 ☐	2 Tim 1:1-10 ☐	1:11-18 ☐	2:1-15 ☐	2:16-26 ☐	3:1-13
77	3:14—4:8 ☐	4:9-22 ☐	Titus 1:1-4 ☐	1:5-16 ☐	2:1-15 ☐	3:1-8 ☐	3:9-15
78	Philem 1:1-11 ☐	1:12-25 ☐	Heb 1:1-2 ☐	1:3-5 ☐	1:6-14 ☐	2:1-9 ☐	2:10-18

Reading Schedule for the Recovery Version of the New Testament with Footnotes

Wk.	Lord's Day	Monday	Tuesday	Wednesday	Thursday	Friday	Saturday
79	Heb 3:1-6 ☐	3:7-19 ☐	4:1-9 ☐	4:10-13 ☐	4:14-16 ☐	5:1-10 ☐	5:11—6:3 ☐
80	6:4-8 ☐	6:9-20 ☐	7:1-10 ☐	7:11-28 ☐	8:1-6 ☐	8:7-13 ☐	9:1-4 ☐
81	9:5-14 ☐	9:15-28 ☐	10:1-18 ☐	10:19-28 ☐	10:29-39 ☐	11:1-6 ☐	11:7-19 ☐
82	11:20-31 ☐	11:32-40 ☐	12:1-2 ☐	12:3-13 ☐	12:14-17 ☐	12:18-26 ☐	12:27-29 ☐
83	13:1-7 ☐	13:8-12 ☐	13:13-15 ☐	13:16-25 ☐	James 1:1-8 ☐	1:9-18 ☐	1:19-27 ☐
84	2:1-13 ☐	2:14-26 ☐	3:1-18 ☐	4:1-10 ☐	4:11-17 ☐	5:1-12 ☐	5:13-20 ☐
85	1 Pet 1:1-2 ☐	1:3-4 ☐	1:5 ☐	1:6-9 ☐	1:10-12 ☐	1:13-17 ☐	1:18-25 ☐
86	2:1-3 ☐	2:4-8 ☐	2:9-17 ☐	2:18-25 ☐	3:1-13 ☐	3:14-22 ☐	4:1-6 ☐
87	4:7-16 ☐	4:17-19 ☐	5:1-4 ☐	5:5-9 ☐	5:10-14 ☐	2 Pet 1:1-2 ☐	1:3-4 ☐
88	1:5-8 ☐	1:9-11 ☐	1:12-18 ☐	1:19-21 ☐	2:1-3 ☐	2:4-11 ☐	2:12-22 ☐
89	3:1-6 ☐	3:7-9 ☐	3:10-12 ☐	3:13-15 ☐	3:16 ☐	3:17-18 ☐	1 John 1:1-2 ☐
90	1:3-4 ☐	1:5 ☐	1:6 ☐	1:7 ☐	1:8-10 ☐	2:1-2 ☐	2:3-11 ☐
91	2:12-14 ☐	2:15-19 ☐	2:20-23 ☐	2:24-27 ☐	2:28-29 ☐	3:1-5 ☐	3:6-10 ☐
92	3:11-18 ☐	3:19-24 ☐	4:1-6 ☐	4:7-11 ☐	4:12-15 ☐	4:16—5:3 ☐	5:4-13 ☐
93	5:14-17 ☐	5:18-21 ☐	2 John 1:1-3 ☐	1:4-9 ☐	1:10-13 ☐	3 John 1:1-6 ☐	1:7-14 ☐
94	Jude 1:1-4 ☐	1:5-10 ☐	1:11-19 ☐	1:20-25 ☐	Rev 1:1-3 ☐	1:4-6 ☐	1:7-11 ☐
95	1:12-13 ☐	1:14-16 ☐	1:17-20 ☐	2:1-6 ☐	2:7 ☐	2:8-9 ☐	2:10-11 ☐
96	2:12-14 ☐	2:15-17 ☐	2:18-23 ☐	2:24-29 ☐	3:1-3 ☐	3:4-6 ☐	3:7-9 ☐
97	3:10-13 ☐	3:14-18 ☐	3:19-22 ☐	4:1-5 ☐	4:6-7 ☐	4:8-11 ☐	5:1-6 ☐
98	5:7-14 ☐	6:1-8 ☐	6:9-17 ☐	7:1-8 ☐	7:9-17 ☐	8:1-6 ☐	8:7-12 ☐
99	8:13—9:11 ☐	9:12-21 ☐	10:1-4 ☐	10:5-11 ☐	11:1-4 ☐	11:5-14 ☐	11:15-19 ☐
100	12:1-4 ☐	12:5-9 ☐	12:10-18 ☐	13:1-10 ☐	13:11-18 ☐	14:1-5 ☐	14:6-12 ☐
101	14:13-20 ☐	15:1-8 ☐	16:1-12 ☐	16:13-21 ☐	17:1-6 ☐	17:7-18 ☐	18:1-8 ☐
102	18:9—19:4 ☐	19:5-10 ☐	19:11-16 ☐	19:17-21 ☐	20:1-6 ☐	20:7-10 ☐	20:11-15 ☐
103	21:1 ☐	21:2 ☐	21:3-8 ☐	21:9-13 ☐	21:14-18 ☐	21:19-21 ☐	21:22-27 ☐
104	22:1 ☐	22:2 ☐	22:3-11 ☐	22:12-15 ☐	22:16-17 ☐	22:18-21 ☐	

Week 13 — Day 6 — Today's verses

Isa. 40:22 It is He who sits above the circle of the earth, and its inhabitants are like grass-hoppers; who stretches out the heavens like a curtain, and spreads them out like a tent to dwell in.

28 Do you not know, or have you not heard, that the eternal God, Jehovah, the Creator of the ends of the earth, does not faint and does not become weary? There is no searching out of His understanding.

_____
Date

Week 13 — Day 5 — Today's verses

Isa. 40:9 Go up to a high mountain, O Zion, who brings glad tidings; lift up your voice with power, O Jerusalem, who brings glad tidings; lift it up, do not be afraid. Say to the cities of Judah, Behold your God!

11 He will feed His flock as a Shepherd; in His arm He will gather the lambs; in His bosom He will carry them. He will lead those who are nursing the young.

_____
Date

Week 13 — Day 4 — Today's verses

Isa. 40:7-8 ...Surely the people are grass. The grass withers and the flower fades, but the word of our God will stand forever.

John 1:1 In the beginning was the Word, and the Word was with God, and the Word was God.

_____
Date

Week 13 — Day 3 — Today's verses

Isa. 40:5 Then the glory of Jehovah will be revealed, and all flesh will see it together, because the mouth of Jehovah has spoken.

2 Cor. 4:6 ...God who said, Out of darkness light shall shine, is the One who shined in our hearts to illuminate the knowledge of the glory of God in the face of Jesus Christ.

_____
Date

Week 13 — Day 2 — Today's verses

Isa. 40:1-3 Comfort, oh, comfort My people, says your God. Speak unto the heart of Jerusalem, and cry out to her...The voice of one who cries in the wilderness: Make clear the way of Jehovah; make straight in the desert a highway for our God.

_____
Date

Week 13 — Day 1 — Today's verses

Exo. 3:14 And God said to Moses, I AM WHO I AM. And He said, Thus you shall say to the children of Israel, I AM has sent me to you.

John 8:58 Jesus said to them, Truly, truly, I say to you, Before Abraham came into being, I am.

_____
Date

Mark
1:2-4

...:"Behold, I send My messenger before Your face, who will prepare Your way; A voice of one crying in the wilderness: Prepare the way of the Lord; make straight His paths." John came baptizing in the wilderness and preaching a baptism of repentance for forgiveness of sins.

Rom.
15:16

That I might be a minister of Christ Jesus to the Gentiles, a laboring priest of the gospel of God, in order that the offering of the Gentiles might be acceptable, having been sanctified in the Holy Spirit.

Isa.
40:29-31

He gives power to the faint, and to those who have no vigor He multiplies strength. Although youths will faint and become weary, and young men will collapse exhausted; yet those who wait on Jehovah will renew *their* strength; they will mount up with wings like eagles; they will run and will not faint; they will walk and will not become weary.

Ezek.
1:9-11

Their wings were joined one to another; they did not turn as they went; each went straight forward. As for the likeness of their faces, *they had* the face of a man; and the four of them had the face of a lion on the right side, and the four of them had the face of an ox on the left side, and the four of them had the face of an eagle. And thus their faces were. And their wings were spread out upward; two *wings* of each were joined one to another, and two covered their bodies.

Isa.
40:3-5

The voice of one who cries in the wilderness: Make clear the way of Jehovah; make straight in the desert a highway for our God. Every valley will be lifted up, and every mountain and hill will be made low, and the crooked places will become straight, and the rough places, a broad plain. Then the glory of Jehovah will be revealed, and all flesh will see *it* together, because the mouth of Jehovah has spoken.

---

2 Kings
2:2

And Elijah said to Elisha, Stay here, for Jehovah has sent me as far as Bethel. And Elisha said, As Jehovah lives and as your soul lives, I will not leave you. So they went down to Bethel.

4

And Elijah said to him, Elisha, stay here, for Jehovah has sent me to Jericho....

6

...Jehovah has sent me to the Jordan....

8

And Elijah took his mantle and wrapped it together and struck the water; and it parted to this side and that, so that the two of them crossed over on dry ground.

Luke
1:17

...It *is* he *who* will go before Him in the spirit and power of Elijah...to prepare for the Lord a people made ready.

4:27

And there were many lepers in Israel during the time of Elisha the prophet, and none of them were cleansed, except Naaman the Syrian.

2 Kings
2:9

...When they had crossed over, Elijah said to Elisha, Ask what I should do for you before I am taken from you. And Elisha said, Let a double portion of your spirit be upon me.

Week 15 — Day 4 Today's verses

Isa. But you, Israel, My servant, Jacob, whom I
41:8 have chosen, the seed of Abraham My
friend.

10 Do not be afraid, for I am with you; do not
be dismayed, for I am your God. I will
strengthen you; surely I will help you;
surely I will uphold you with the right
hand of My righteousness.

43:7 Everyone who is called by My name,
whom I have created, formed, and even
made for My glory.

Date

Week 15 — Day 5 Today's verses

Isa. And He has made my mouth like a sharp
49:2-4 sword...And He said to me, You are My
servant, Israel, in whom I will be glorified.
But I said, I have labored in vain; I have
used up my strength for nothing and vanity; yet surely the justice *due* to me is with
Jehovah, and my recompense with my
God.

Date

Week 15 — Day 6 Today's verses

Isa. The Lord Jehovah has given me the
50:4-5 tongue of the instructed, that I should
know how to sustain the weary with a
word. He awakens *me* morning by morning; He awakens my ear to hear as an instructed one. The Lord Jehovah has
opened my ear; and I was not rebellious,
nor did I turn back.

Date

Week 15 — Day 1 Today's verses

Isa. The Spirit of the Lord Jehovah is upon Me,
61:1-2 because Jehovah has anointed Me to
bring good news to the afflicted; He has
sent Me to bind up *the wounds* of the brokenhearted, to proclaim liberty to the
captives, and the opening *of the eyes* to
those who are bound; to proclaim the acceptable year of Jehovah and the day of
vengeance of our God; to comfort all who
mourn.

Date

Week 15 — Day 2 Today's verses

Isa. Come out from Babylon; flee from the
48:20 Chaldeans; with a voice of shouting declare; let them hear this, send it out unto
the end of the earth; say, Jehovah has redeemed His servant Jacob.

Rom. ...The kingdom of God is not eating and
14:17 drinking, but righteousness and peace
and joy in the Holy Spirit.

Date

Week 15 — Day 3 Today's verses

Isa. [Thus says Jehovah] who says to Cyrus,
44:28 *He is* My shepherd, and he will fulfill all
My desire, even by saying of Jerusalem,
She will be built, and of the temple, *Her
foundations* will be laid.

48:14 Assemble yourselves, all of you, and
hear! Who among them has declared
these things? Jehovah loves him; he will
do His pleasure on Babylon, and His arm
will be upon the Chaldeans.

Date

Week 16 — Day 4   Today's verses

Isa. The Lord Jehovah has given me the tongue
50:4-5 of the instructed, that I should know how
to sustain the weary with a word. He
awakens *me* morning by morning; He
awakens my ear to hear as an instructed
one. The Lord Jehovah has opened my
ear; and I was not rebellious, nor did I turn
back.

Date

Week 16 — Day 5   Today's verses

Isa. I am Jehovah, that is My name, and I will
42:8 not give My glory to another, nor My
praise to idols.

1 John And we know that the Son of God has
5:20-21 come and has given us an understanding
that we might know Him who is true; and
we are in Him who is true, in His Son
Jesus Christ. This is the true God and eternal life. Little children, guard yourselves
from idols.

Date

Week 16 — Day 6   Today's verses

Isa. You are My witnesses, declares Jehovah,
43:10-11 and My servant whom I have chosen, in
order that you may know and believe Me
and understand that I am He. Before Me
there was no God formed, neither will
there be any after Me. I, *even* I, am Jehovah; and there is no Savior besides Me.

Date

Week 16 — Day 1   Today's verses

Isa. Here is My Servant, whom I uphold, My
42:1 chosen One *in whom* My soul delights;
I have put My Spirit upon Him, and He
will bring forth justice to the nations.

4 He will not faint, nor will He be discouraged, until He has established justice in
the earth...

52:13 Indeed, My Servant will act wisely and
will prosper; He will be exalted and lifted
up and very high.

Date

Week 16 — Day 2   Today's verses

Matt. "Behold, My Servant whom I have cho-
12:18-19 sen, My Beloved in whom My soul has
found delight. I will put My Spirit upon
Him, and He will announce justice to the
Gentiles. He will not strive nor cry out,
nor will anyone hear His voice in the
streets."

Date

Week 16 — Day 3   Today's verses

Isa. I gave my back to those who strike *me* and
50:6 my cheeks to those who pluck out *the
hair;* I did not hide my face from humiliation and spitting.

53:6 We all like sheep have gone astray; each
of us has turned to his own way, and Jehovah has caused the iniquity of us all to fall
on Him.

Date

Week 17 — Day 4 | Today's verses

Isa. He will not faint, nor will He be discour-
42:4 aged, until He has established justice in
the earth...

Isa. But I said, I have labored in vain; I have
49:4 used up my strength for nothing and vanity; yet surely the justice *due* to me is with
Jehovah, and my recompense with my
God.

Date _____

Week 17 — Day 5 | Today's verses

Isa. Even as many were astonished at Him—
52:14-15 His visage was marred more than that of
any man, and His form more than that of
the sons of men—so will He surprise
many nations; kings will shut their
mouths because of Him; for what had not
been recounted to them they will see, and
what they had not heard of they will contemplate.

Date _____

Week 17 — Day 6 | Today's verses

Mark And He...came into His own country...
6:1-4 And when the Sabbath had come, He
began to teach in the synagogue; and
many hearing were astounded, saying,
Where *did* this man get these things?...Is
not this the carpenter?...And they were
stumbled because of Him. And Jesus said
to them, A prophet is not without honor
except in his *own* country and among his
own relatives and in his *own* house.

Date _____

Week 17 — Day 1 | Today's verses

Rom. ...God, sending His own Son in the like-
8:3 ness of the flesh of sin and concerning sin,
condemned sin in the flesh.

1 John In this the love of God was manifested
4:9 among us, that God sent His only begotten Son into the world that we might have
life and live through Him.

15 Whoever confesses that Jesus is the Son of
God, God abides in him and he in God.

Date _____

Week 17 — Day 2 | Today's verses

Isa. Who has believed our report? And to
53:1-3 whom has the arm of Jehovah been revealed? For He grew up like a tender plant
before Him, and like a root out of dry
ground...He was despised and forsaken
of men, a man of sorrows...

1 Cor. ...We preach Christ crucified, to Jews a
1:23-24 stumbling block, and to Gentiles foolishness, but to those who are called, both
Jews and Greeks, Christ the power of God
and the wisdom of God.

Date _____

Week 17 — Day 3 | Today's verses

Isa. He has no *attracting* form nor majesty that
53:2-3 we should look upon Him, nor beautiful
appearance that we should desire Him.
He was despised and forsaken of men, a
man of sorrows and acquainted with
grief; and like one from whom *men* hide
their faces, He was despised; and we did
not esteem Him.

Date _____

Week 18 — Day 1

Today's verses

Isa. Surely He has borne our sicknesses, and
53:4-5 carried our sorrows; yet we ourselves esteemed Him stricken, smitten of God and afflicted. But He was wounded because of our transgressions; He was crushed because of our iniquities; the chastening for our peace was upon Him, and by His stripes we have been healed.

Week 18 — Day 2

Today's verses

1 Pet. Who Himself bore up our sins in His body
2:24-25 on the tree, in order that we, having died to sins, might live to righteousness; by whose bruise you were healed. For you were like sheep being led astray, but you have now returned to the Shepherd and Overseer of your souls.

Week 18 — Day 3

Today's verses

Isa. We all like sheep have gone astray; each
53:6 of us has turned to his own way, and Jehovah has caused the iniquity of us all to fall on Him.

Exo. Do not eat any of it raw or boiled at all
12:9 with water, but roasted with fire—its head with its legs and with its inward parts.

Week 18 — Day 4

Today's verses

Rom. For if we, being enemies, were reconciled
5:10 to God through the death of His Son, much more we will be saved in His life, having been reconciled.

Isa. He was oppressed, and it was He who
53:7 was afflicted, yet He did not open His mouth; like a lamb that is led to the slaughter and like a sheep that is dumb before its shearers, so He did not open His mouth.

Week 18 — Day 5

Today's verses

Isa. And they assigned His grave with the
53:9-10 wicked, but with a rich man in His death, although He had done no violence, nor was there any deceit in His mouth. But Jehovah was pleased to crush Him, to afflict Him with grief. When He makes Himself an offering for sin...

Heb. Having therefore, brothers, boldness for
10:19 entering the *Holy of Holies* in the blood of Jesus.

Week 18 — Day 6

Today's verses

John But one of the soldiers pierced His side
19:34 with a spear, and immediately there came out blood and water.

Isa. ...Because He poured out His life unto
53:12 death and was numbered with the transgressors, yet He alone bore the sin of many and interceded for the transgressors.

Luke And Jesus said, Father, forgive them, for
23:34 they do not know what they are doing....